COLOR

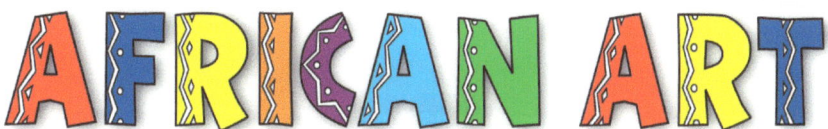
AFRICAN ART

I0467337

Conceived, Designed, and Illustrated by:

Mrinal Mitra

Series Edited by:

Swarna Mitra & Malika Mitra

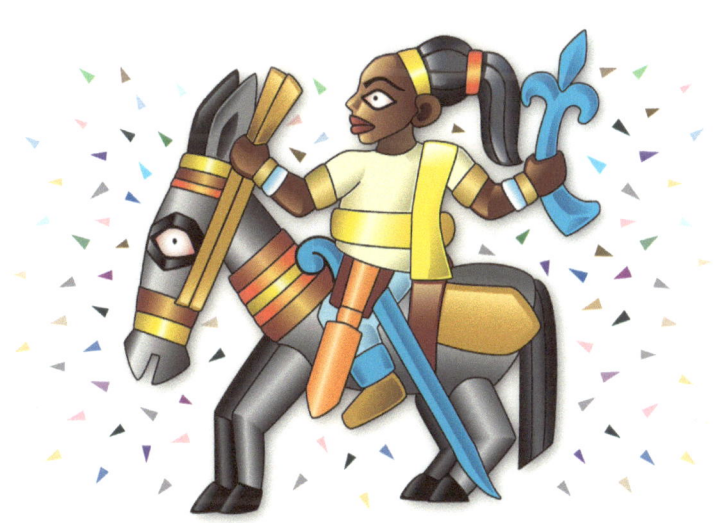

WORLD CULTURE COLORING SERIES

*This series is dedicated to the citizens of the world;
from the young blooming minds of children, to the aspired individuals of all ages.*

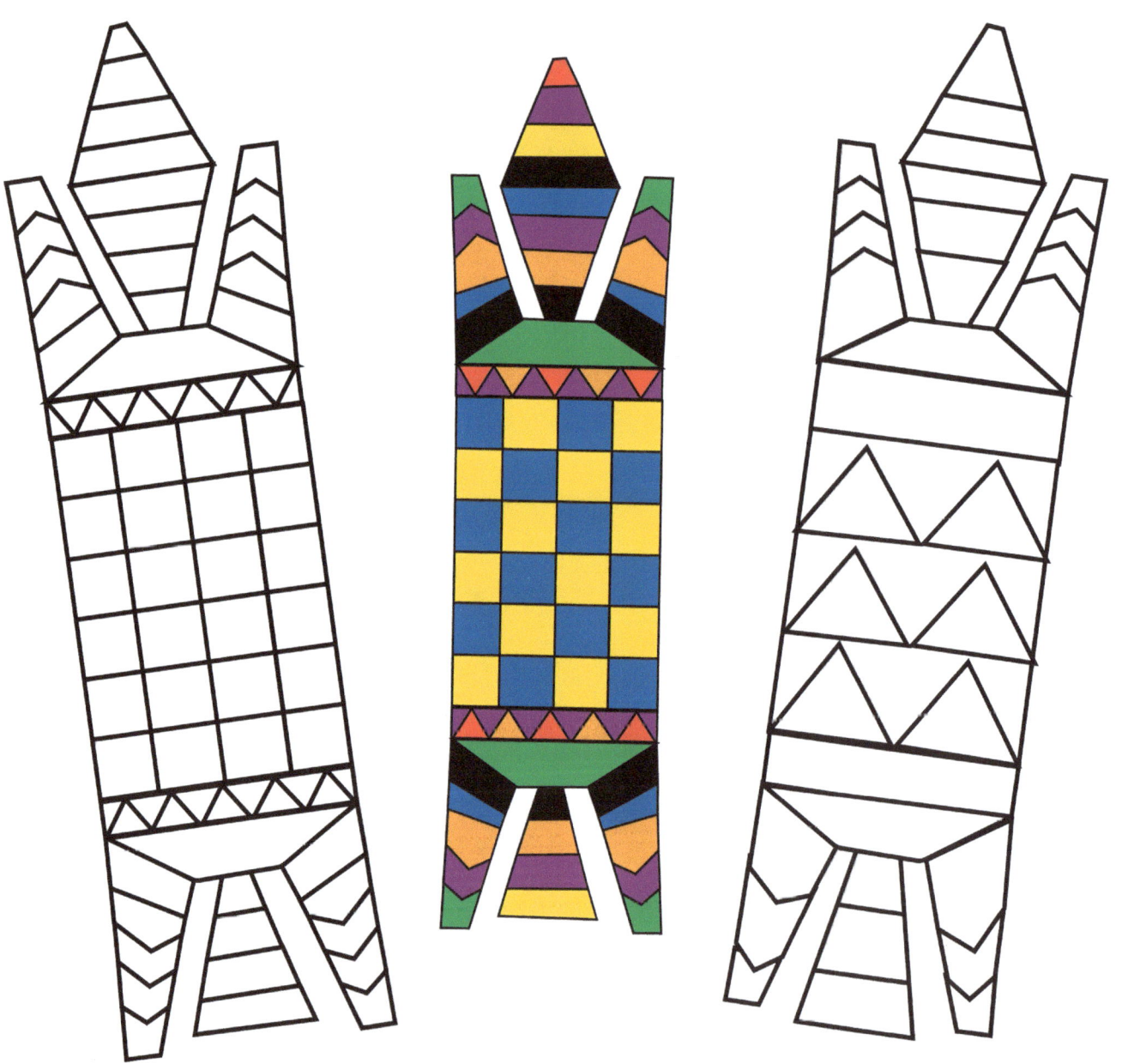

Part of a dance mask on Do the Guardian Spirit.
Bobo, Upper Volta (Burkina Faso). These masks are worn by
groups of youth after sowing.

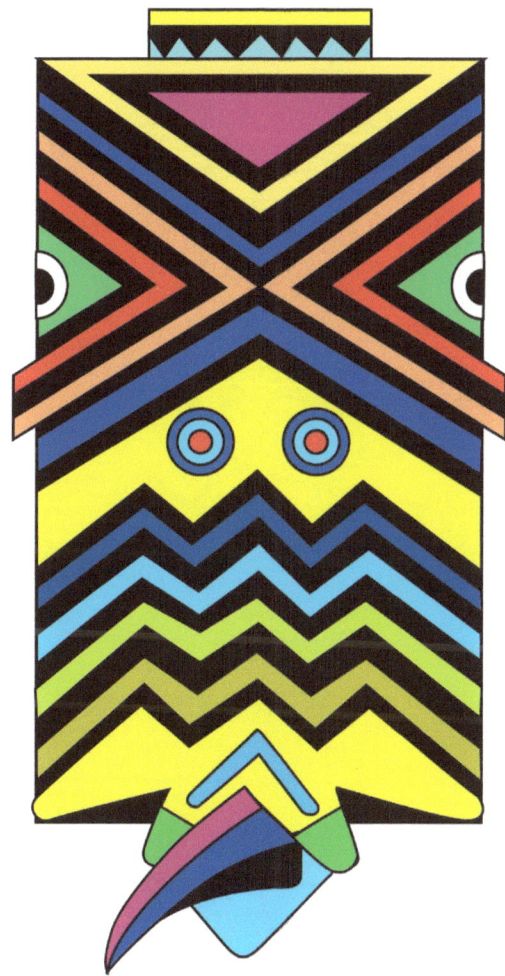

Bird mask. Wood.
Bobo, Dioulasso region.
Upper Volta (Barkina Faso).

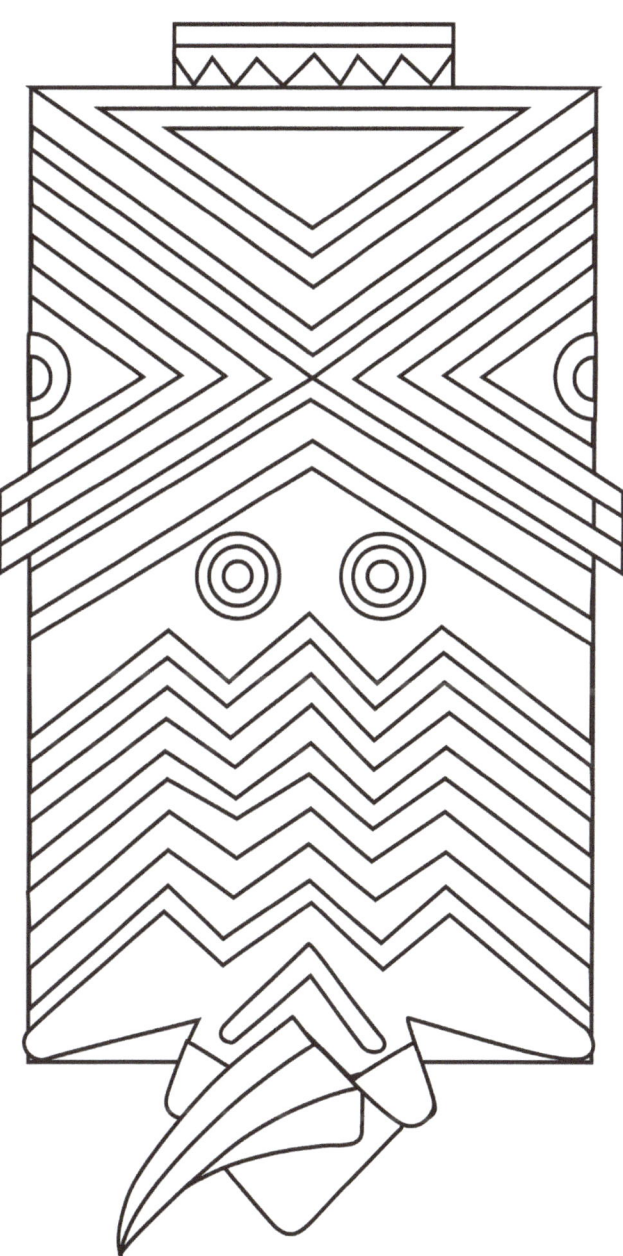

Color the drawings above using your preferred choice of colors.

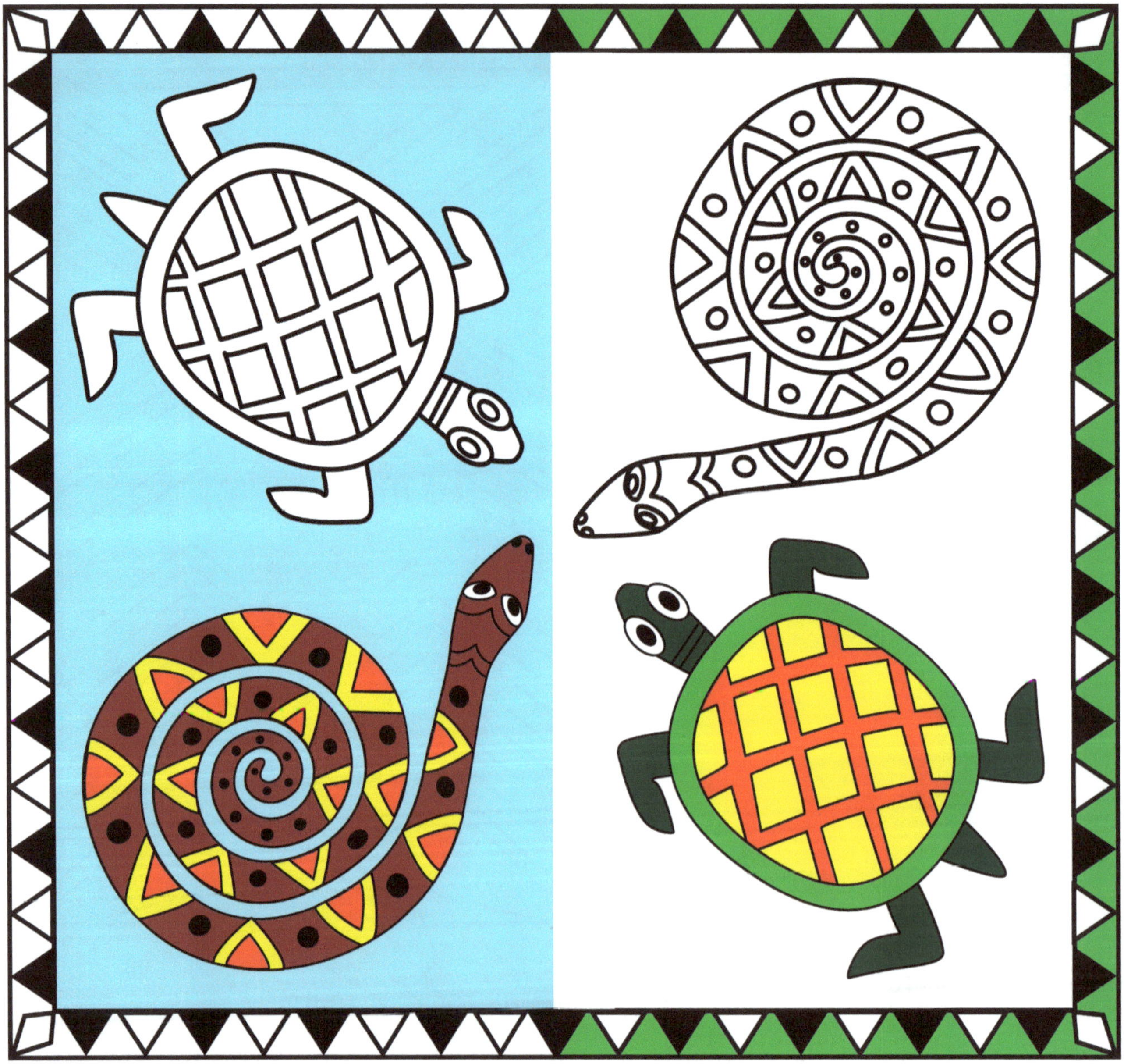

Coiled snakes and turtles on a frieze found in a palace door in Yoruba, Nigeria.

African Art

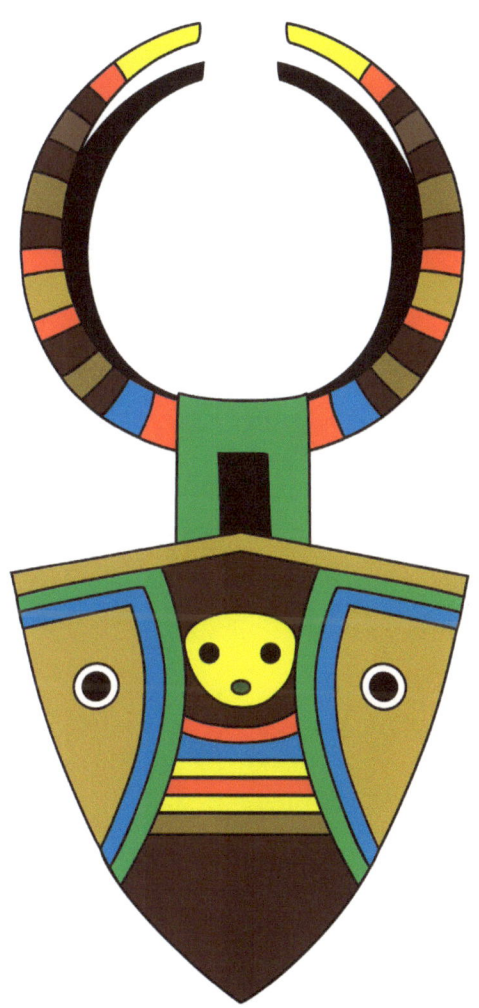

Sakrobundi mask.
Wood with colored decoration.
Northern region of Ghana.

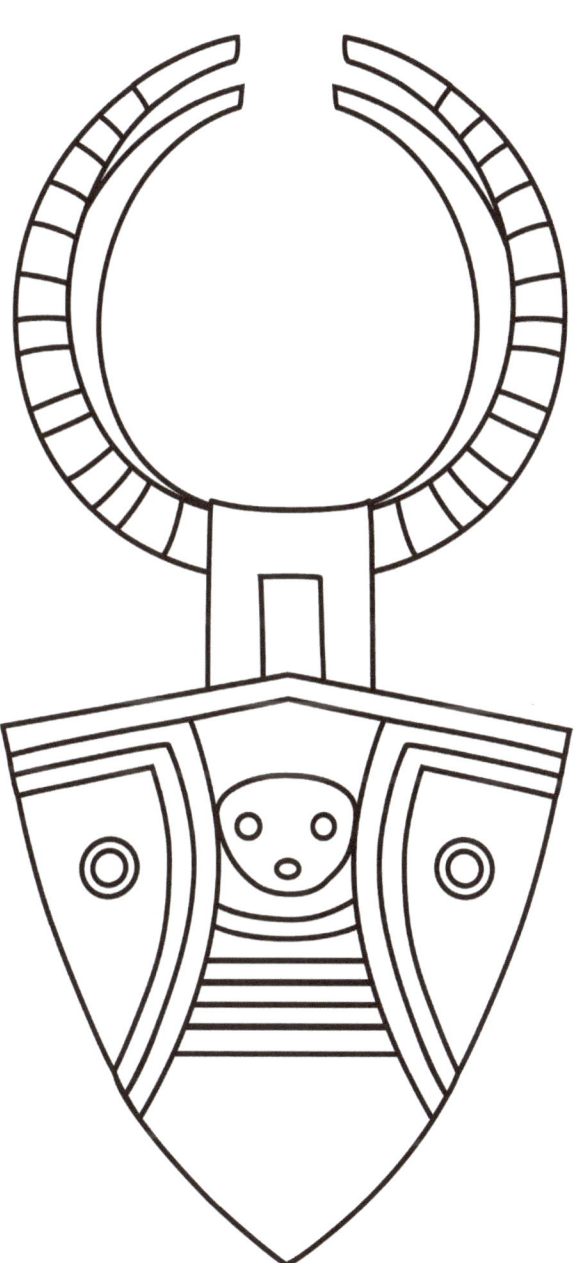

Color the drawings above using your preferred choice of colors.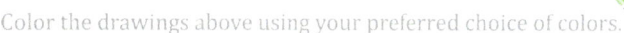

5

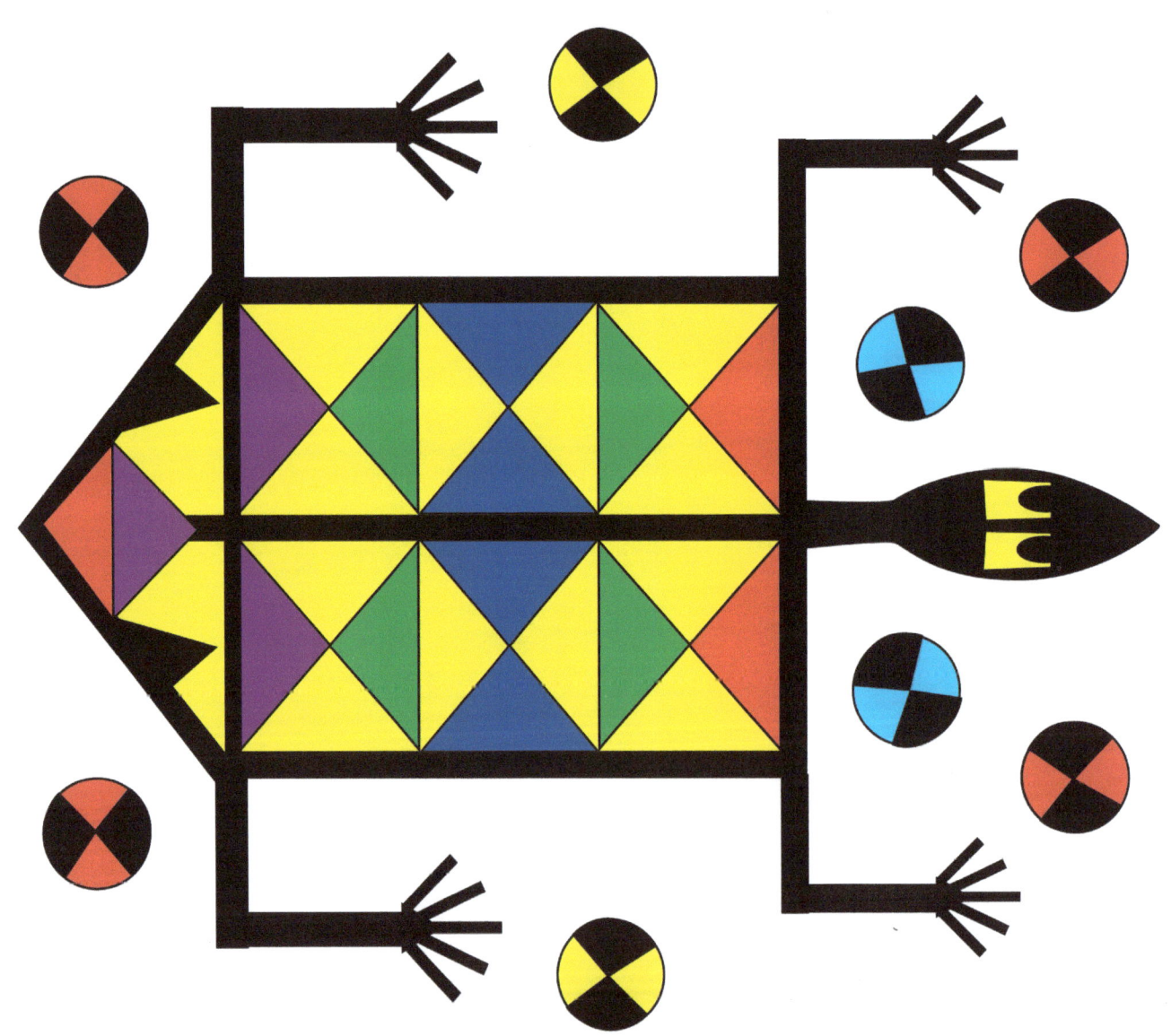

Hand painted Senufo cloth showing wild animal,
Cote d'Ivoire (Ivory Coast).

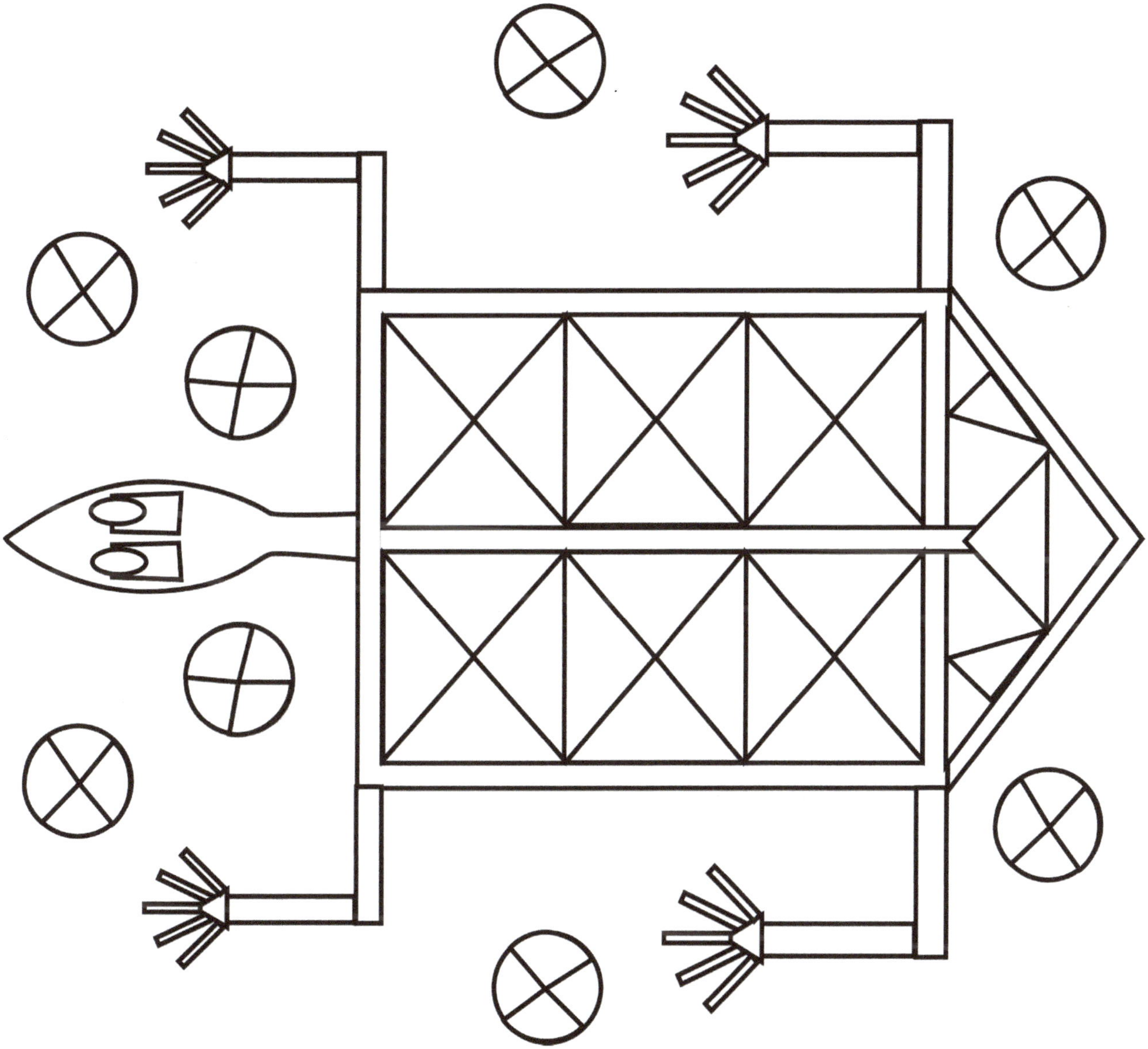

Color the drawing above using your preferred choice of colors.

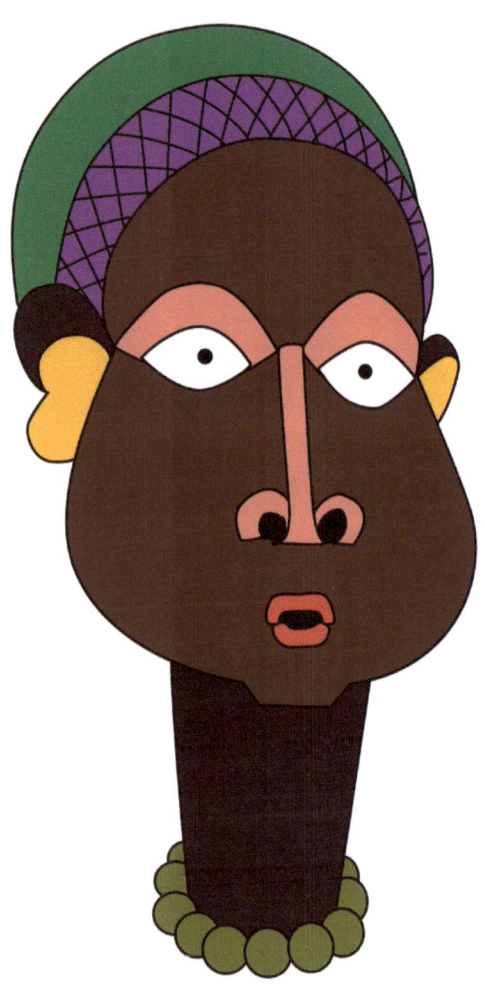

Ancestral memorial.
Made by the Wabembe tribe.
Basikasingo, Congo.

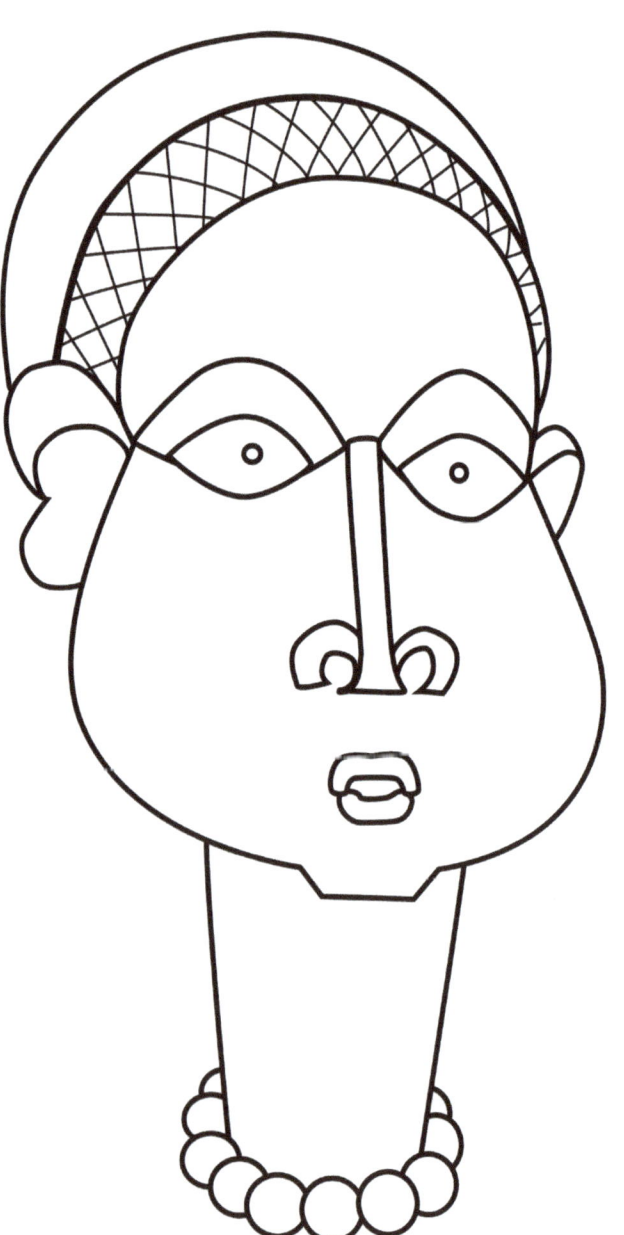

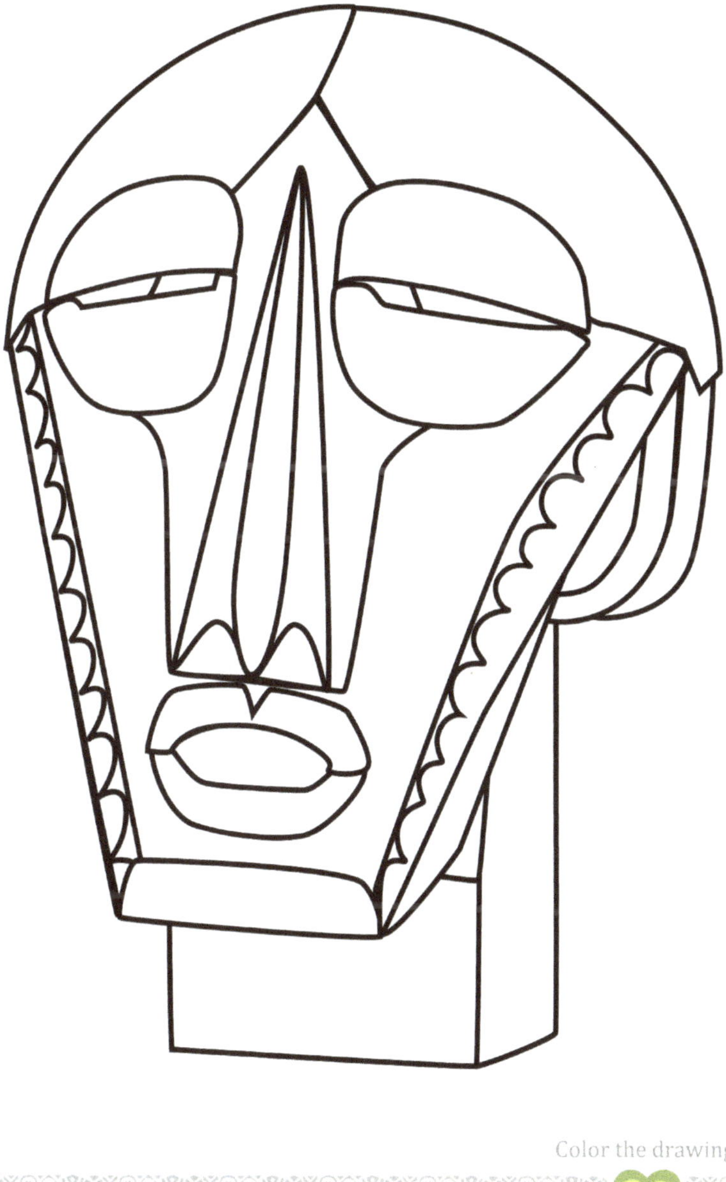

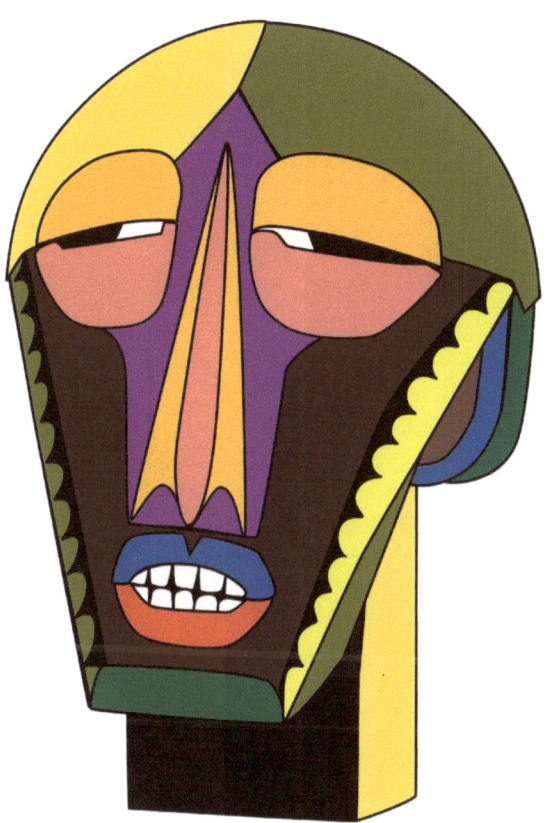

Ancestral memorial.
Made by the Wabembe tribe.
Basikasingo, Congo.

Color the drawings above using your preferred choice of colors.

9
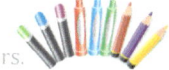

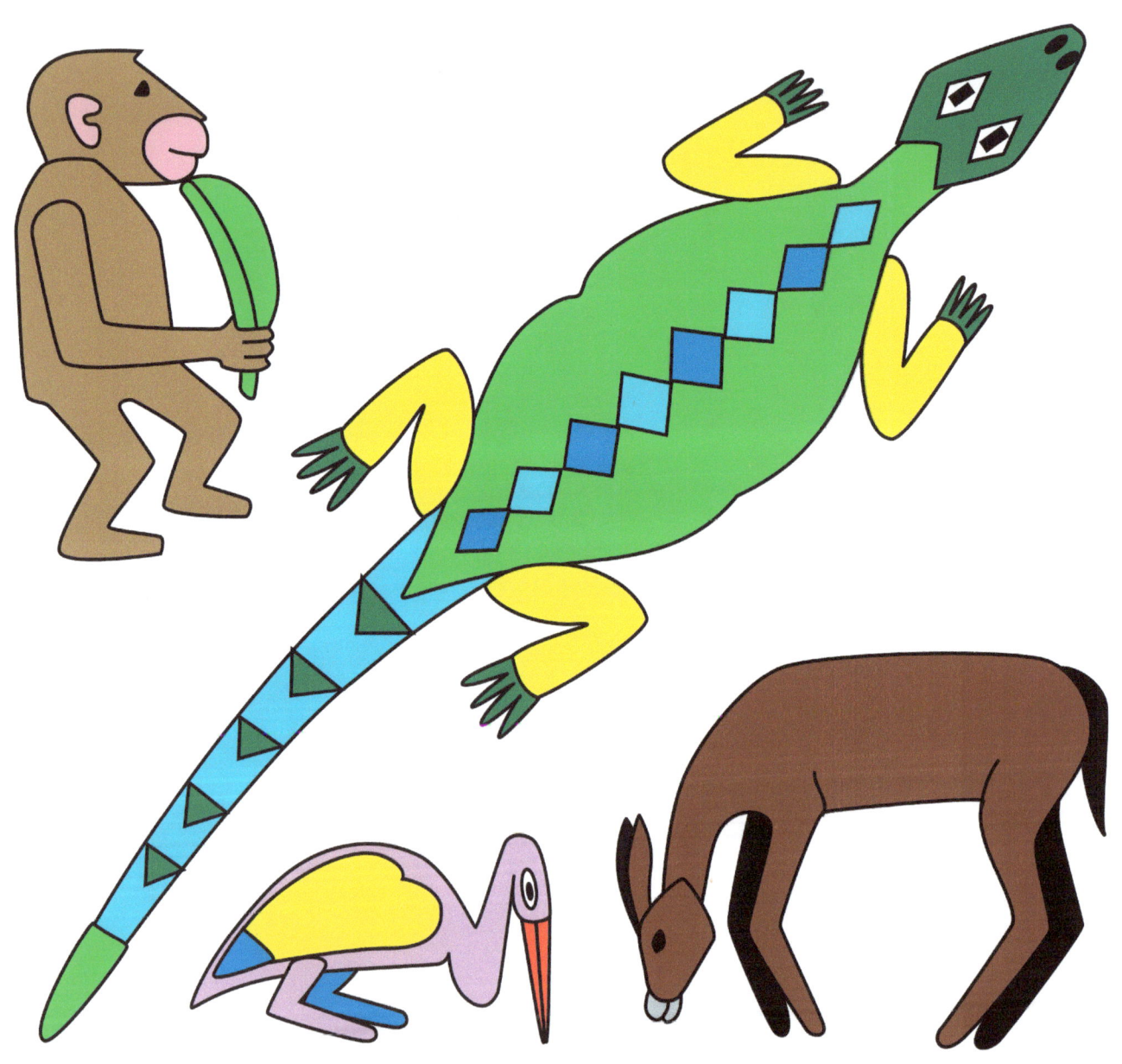

Animal motifs from a granary door, Senufo.
Woodwork, Northern Cote d'Ivoire (Ivory Coast).

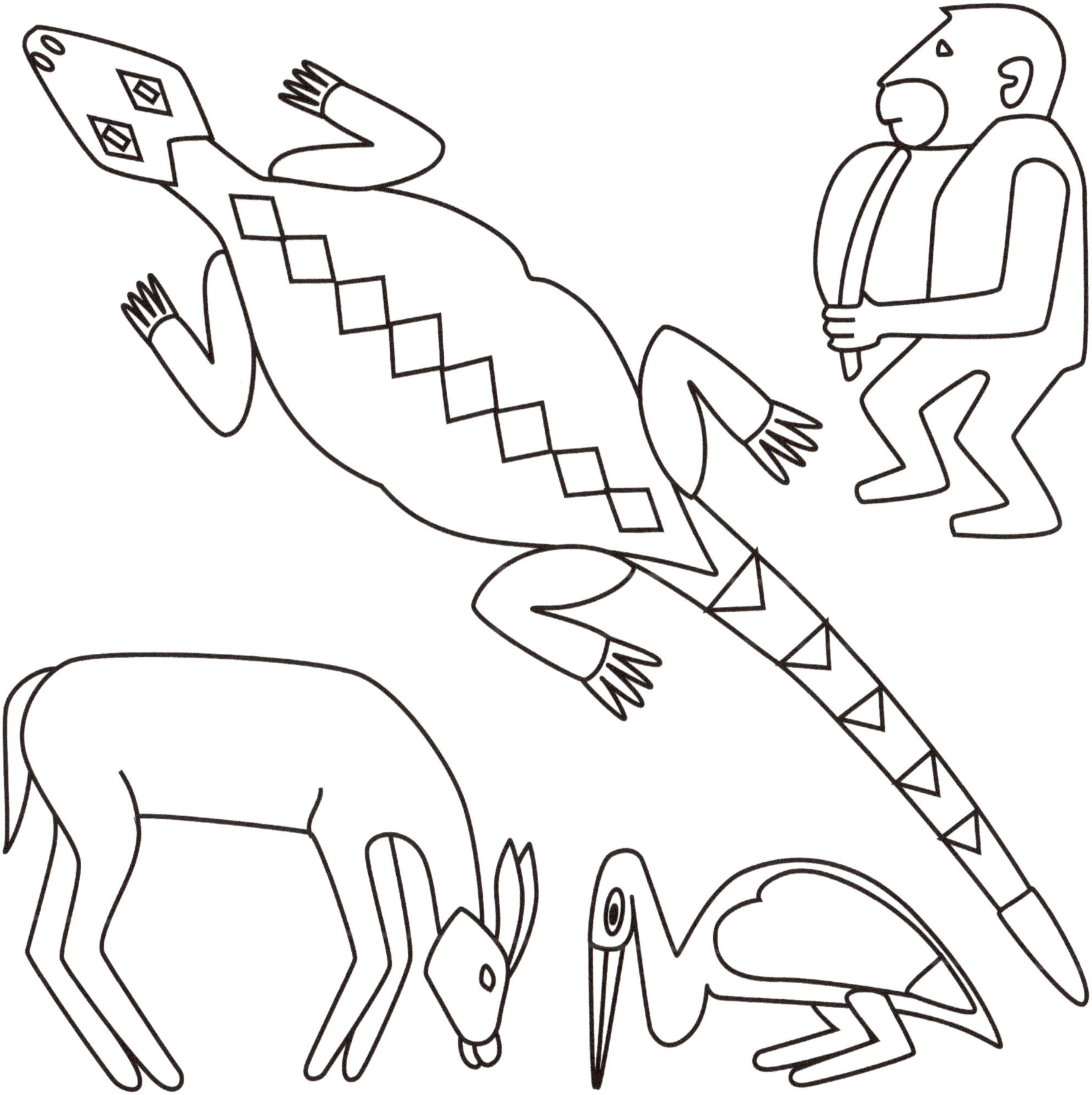

Color the drawings above using your preferred choice of colors.

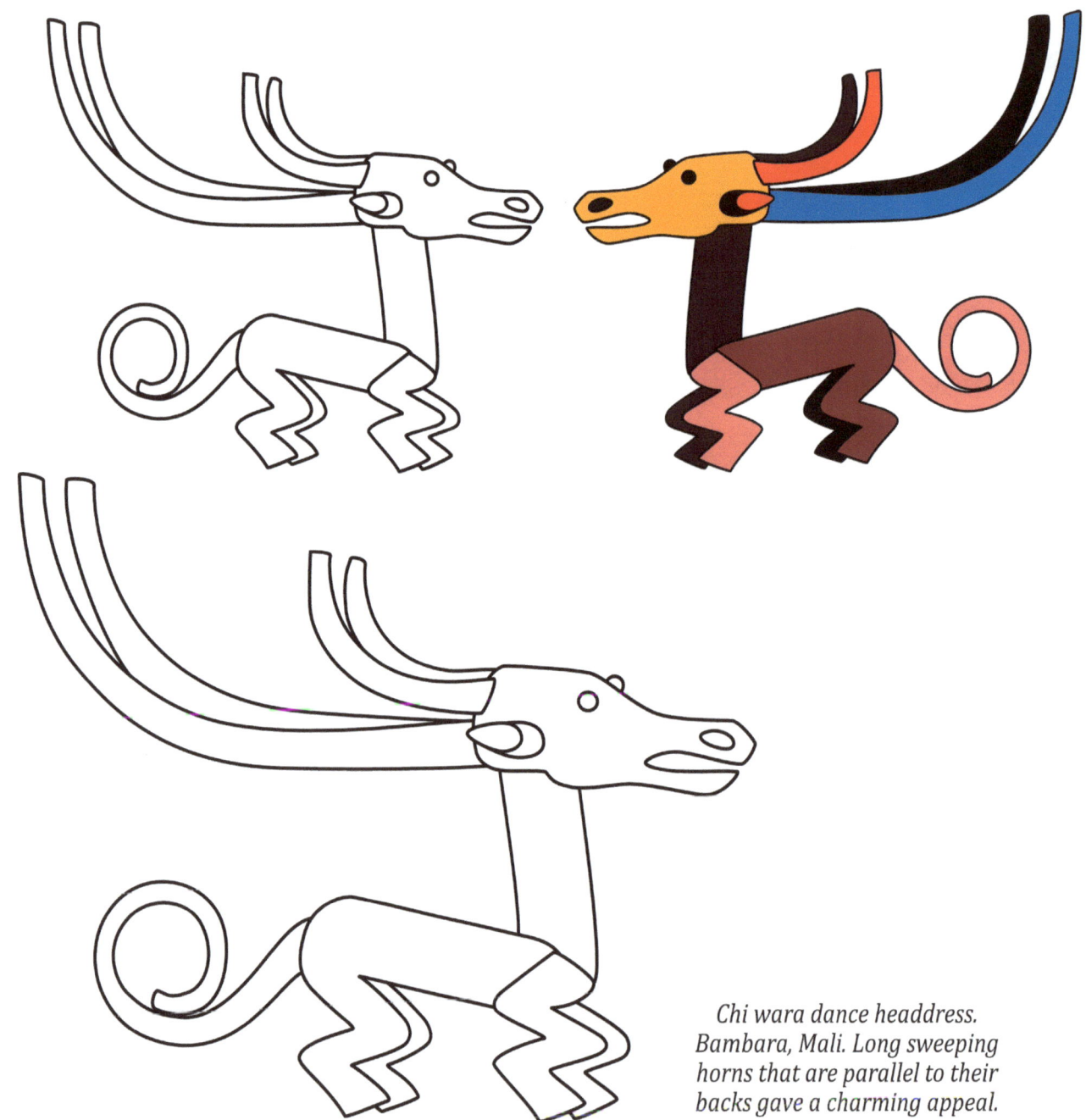

Chi wara dance headdress. Bambara, Mali. Long sweeping horns that are parallel to their backs gave a charming appeal.

African Art

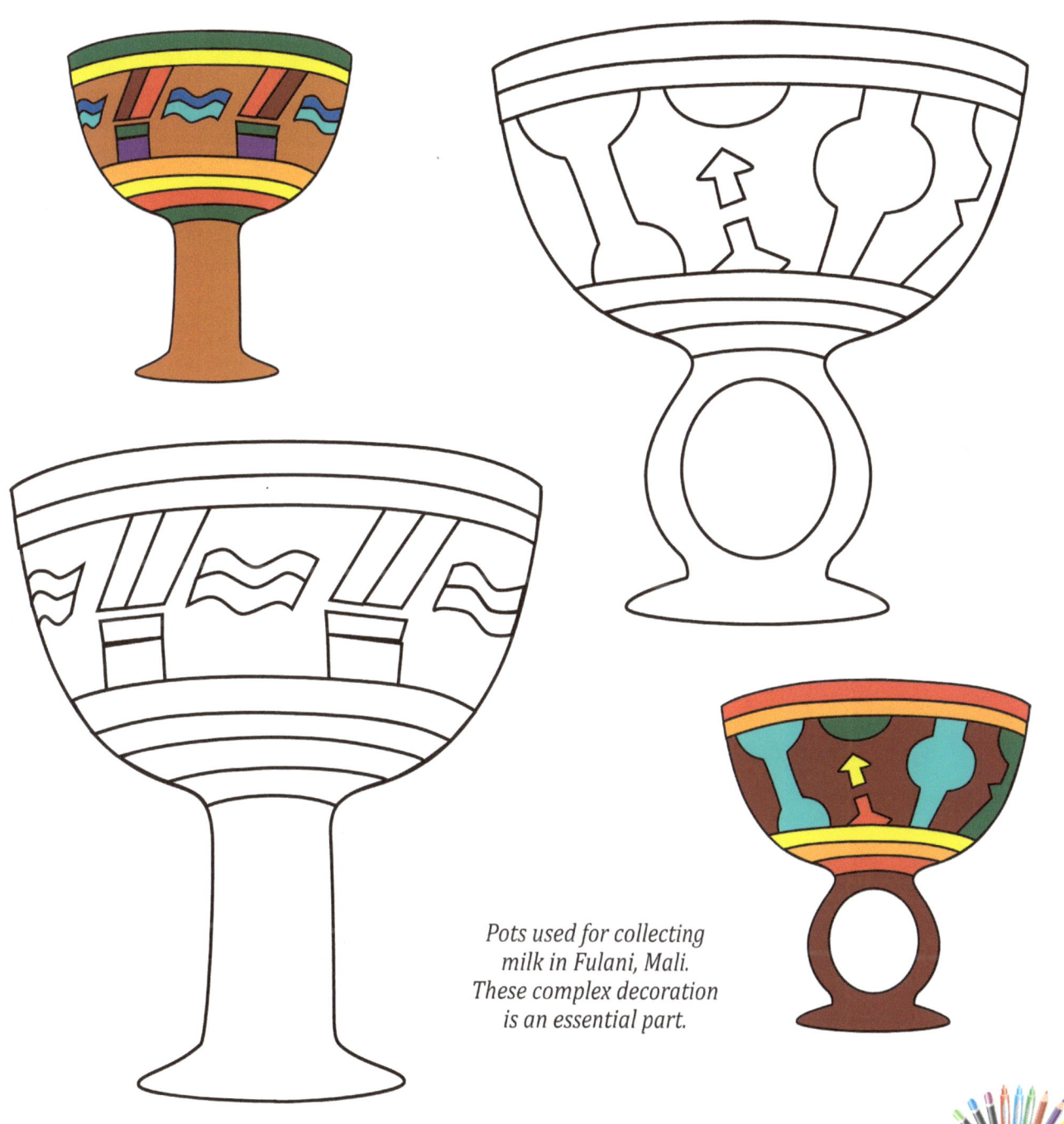

Pots used for collecting milk in Fulani, Mali. These complex decoration is an essential part.

Color the drawings above using your preferred choice of colors.

13

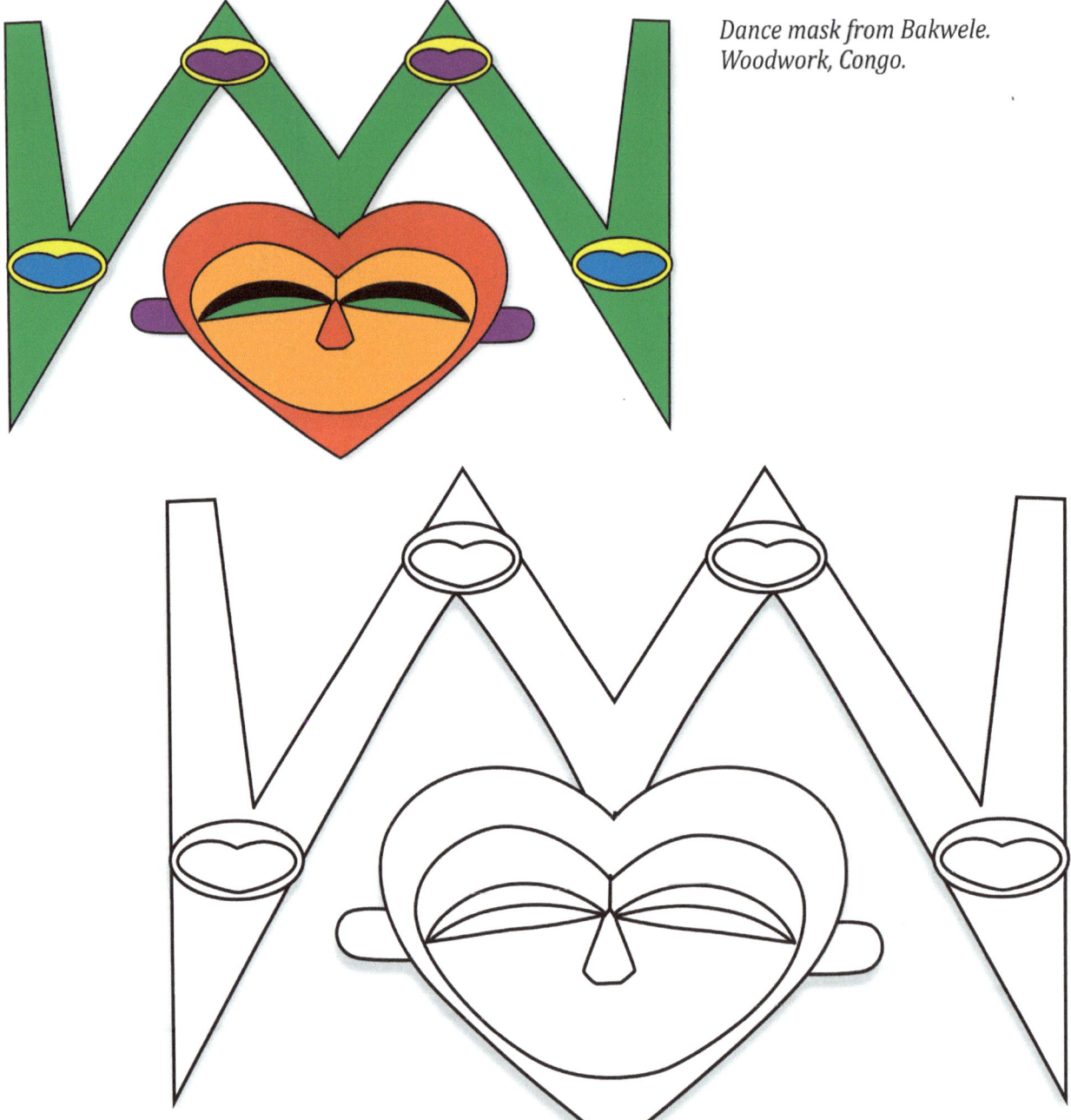

Dance mask from Bakwele.
Woodwork, Congo.

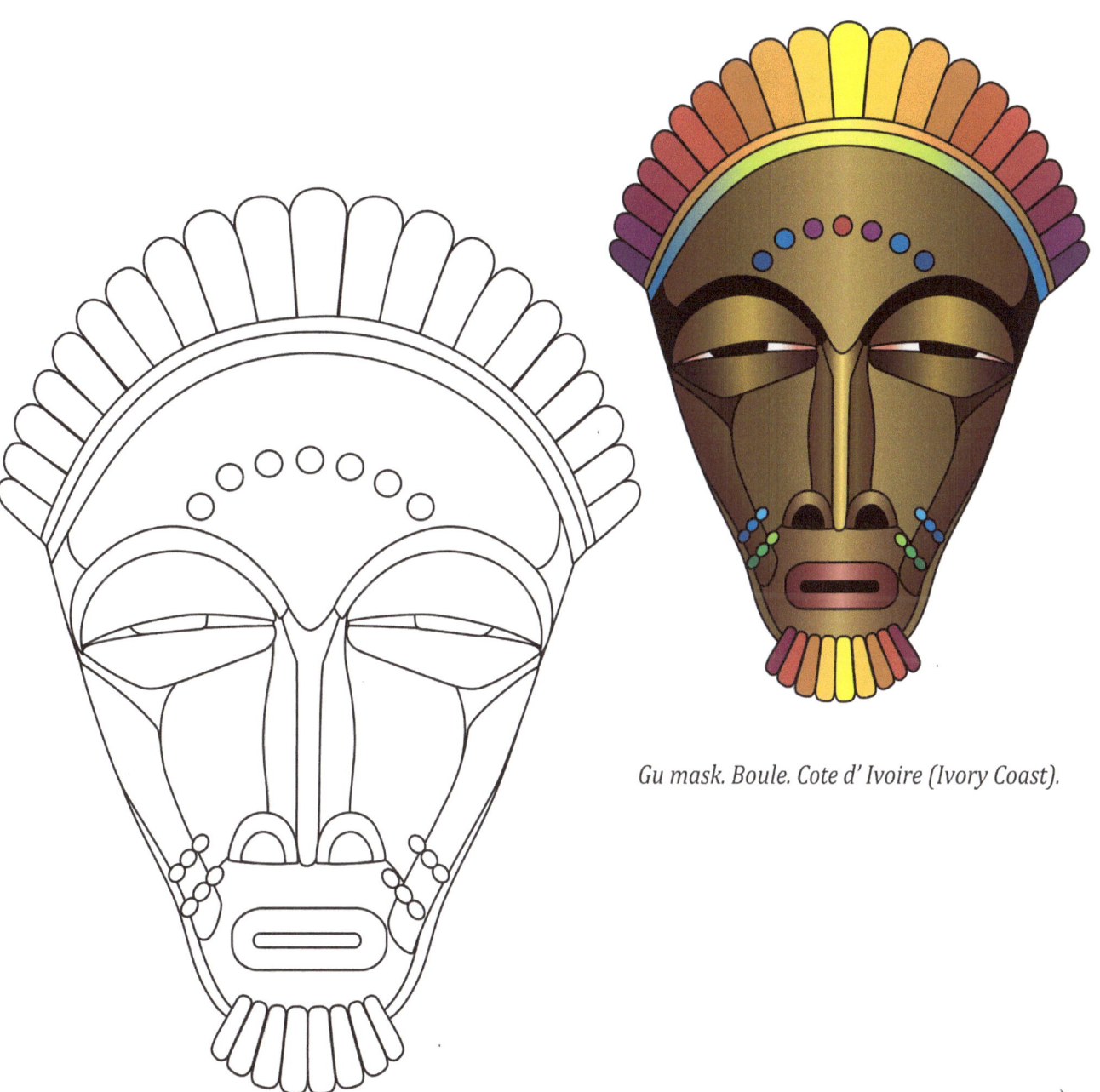

Gu mask. Boule. Cote d' Ivoire (Ivory Coast).

Color the drawings above using your preferred choice of colors.

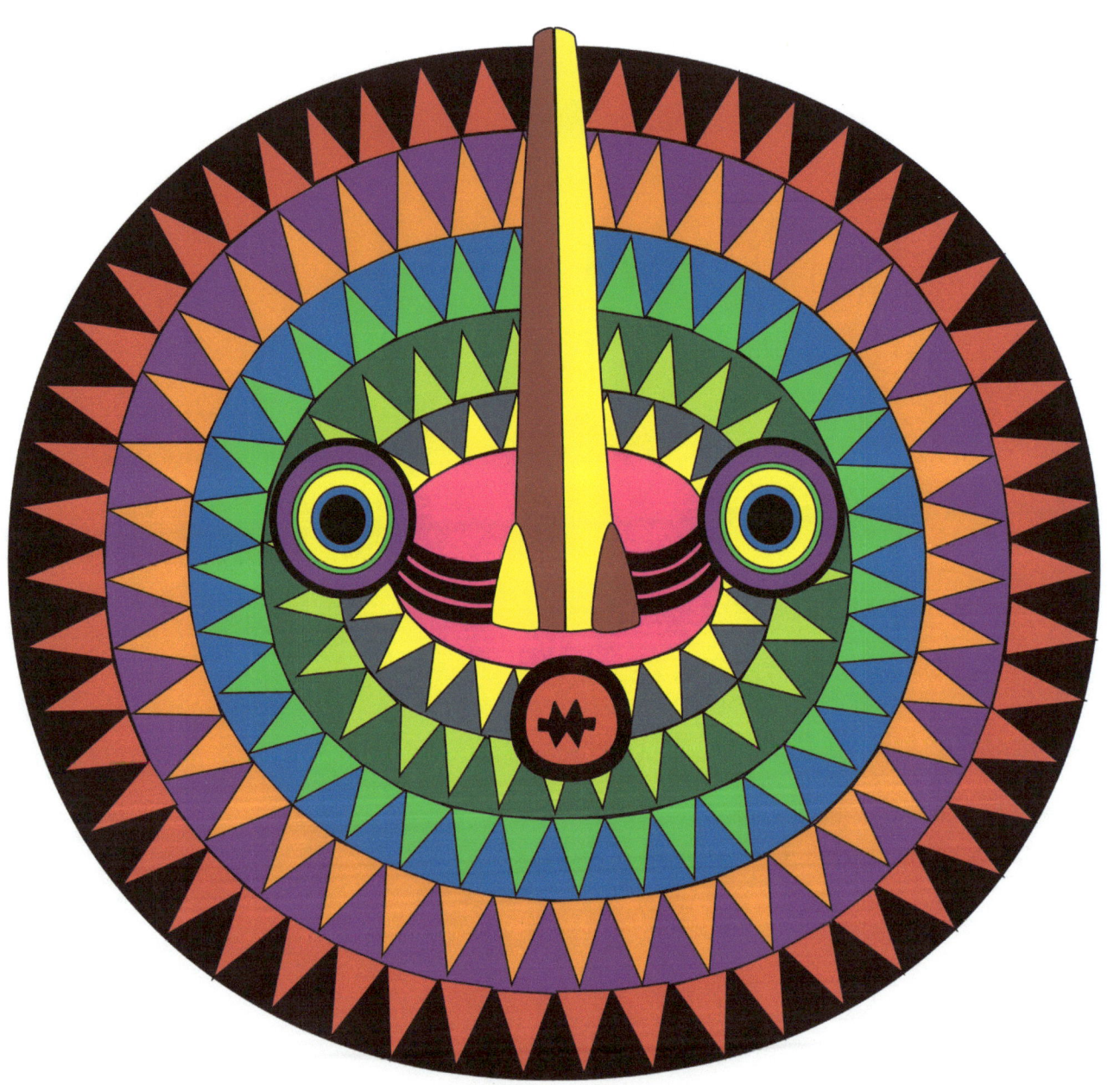

The Bobo population from Burkina Faso, Africa, carve circular masks like this on wood to represent owls and other birds. These masks are worn for performative rituals.

African Art

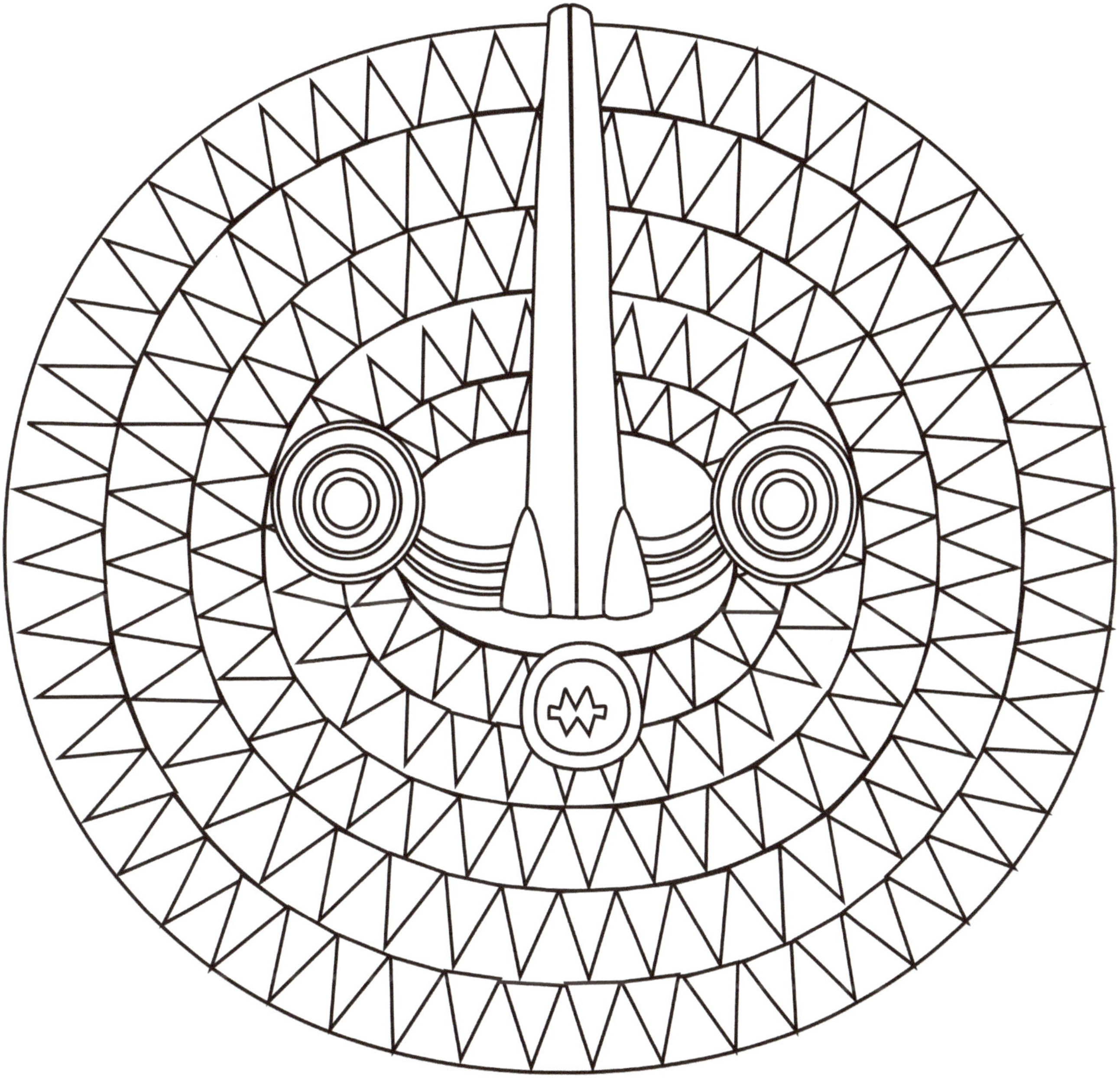

Color the drawing above using your preferred choice of colors.

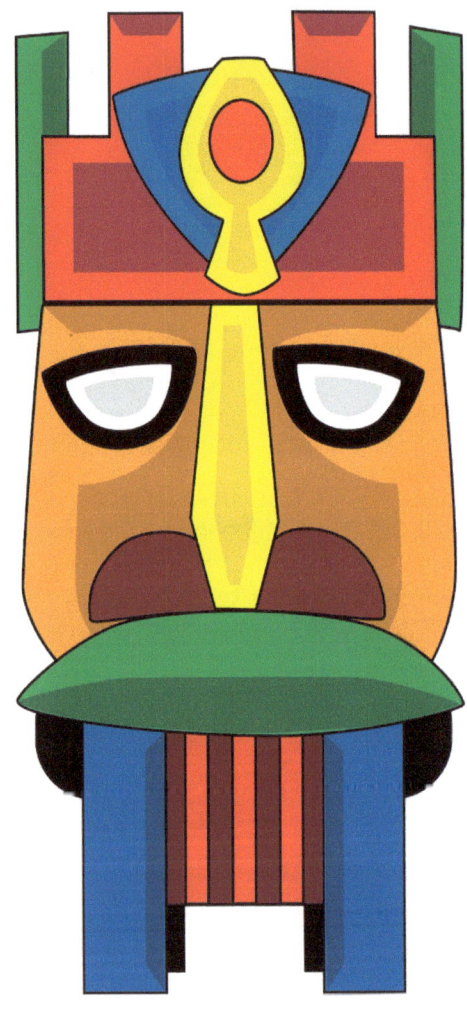

Mask of the Water Spirit.
Woodwork, Nigeria.

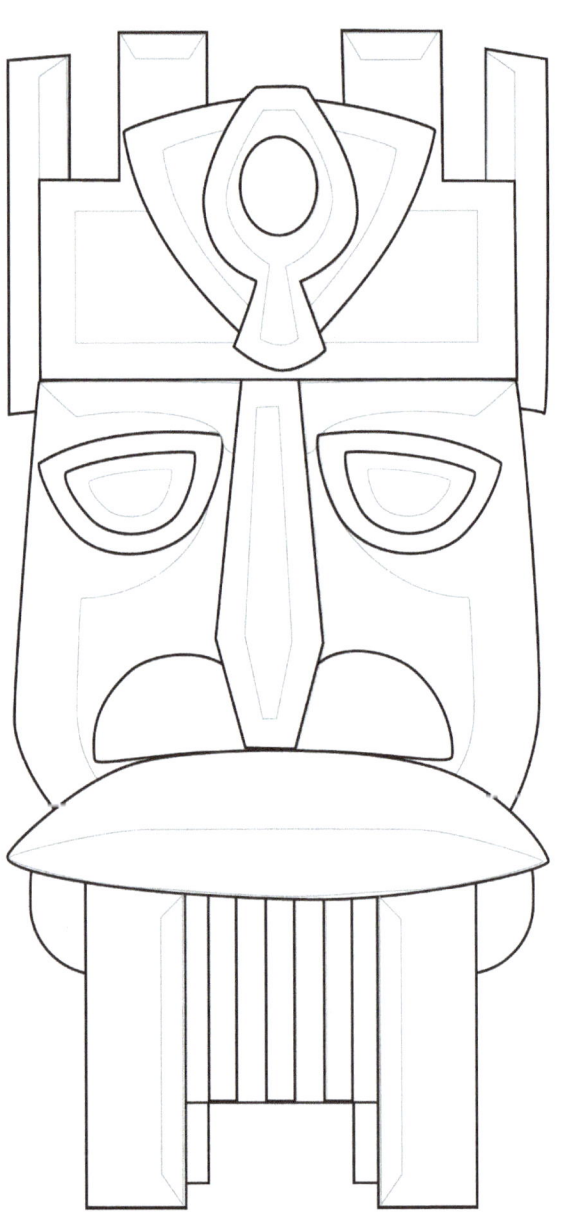

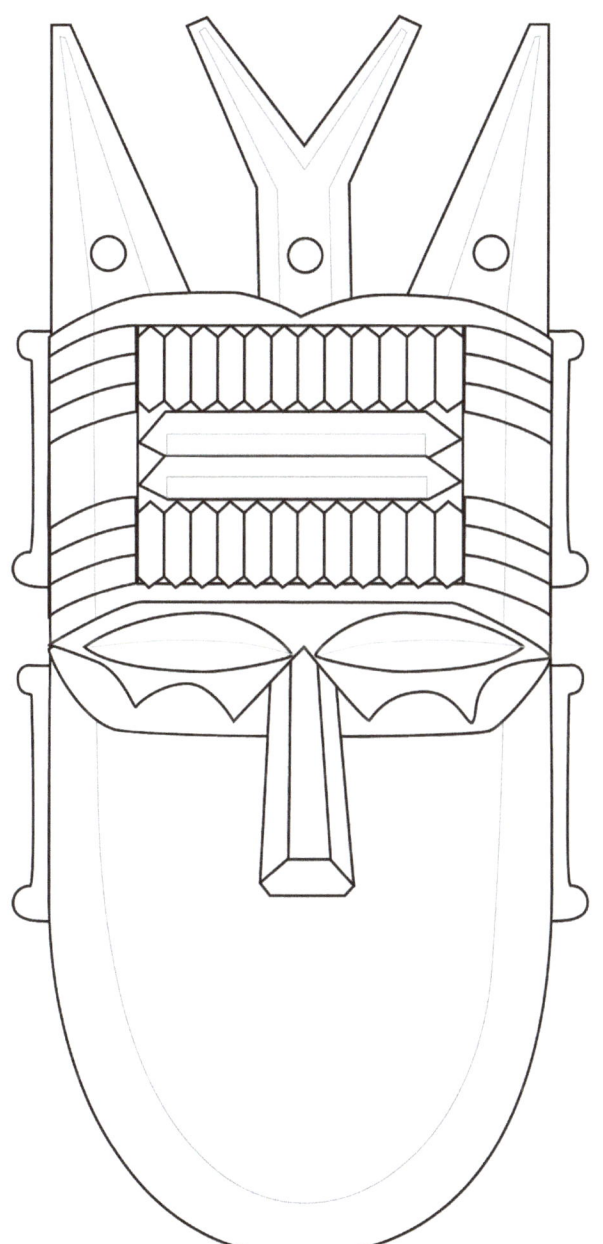

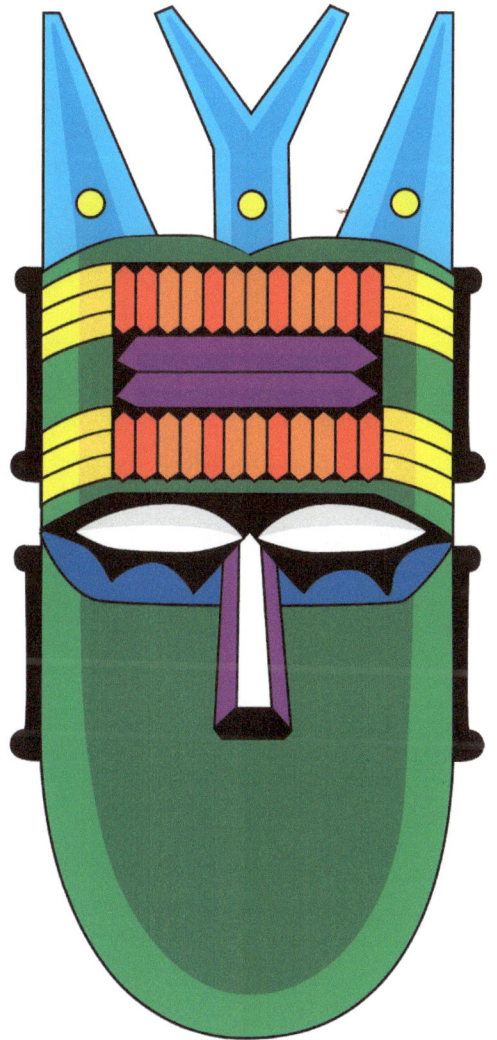

Mask of the Poro Society.
Woodwork, Toma, Guinea Coast.

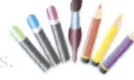

Color the drawings above using your preferred choice of colors.

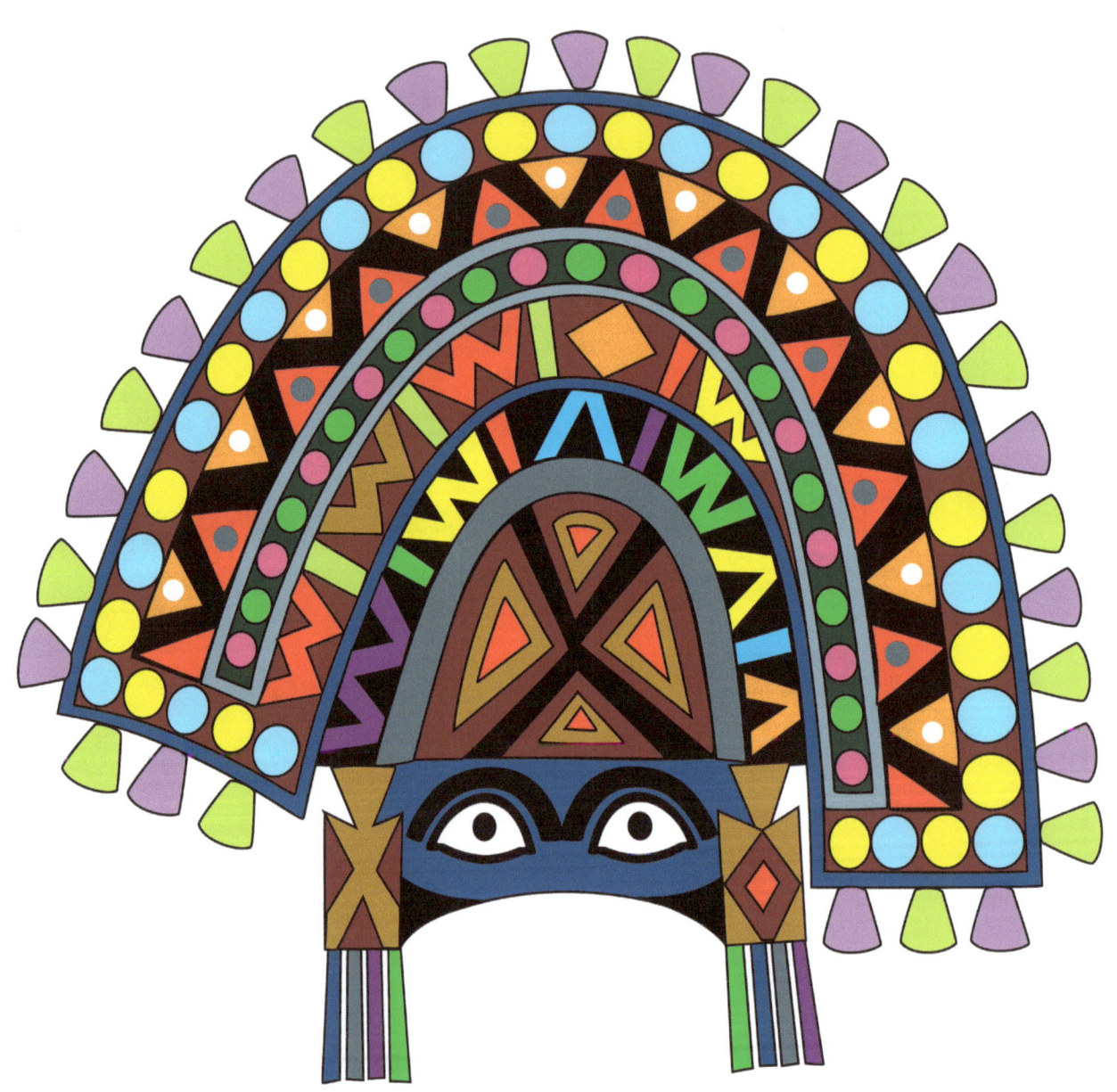

Part of a Crested mask of the
Mmwo Society (cult of the female ancestral spirits). Igbo (Ibo). Woodwork. Nigeria.

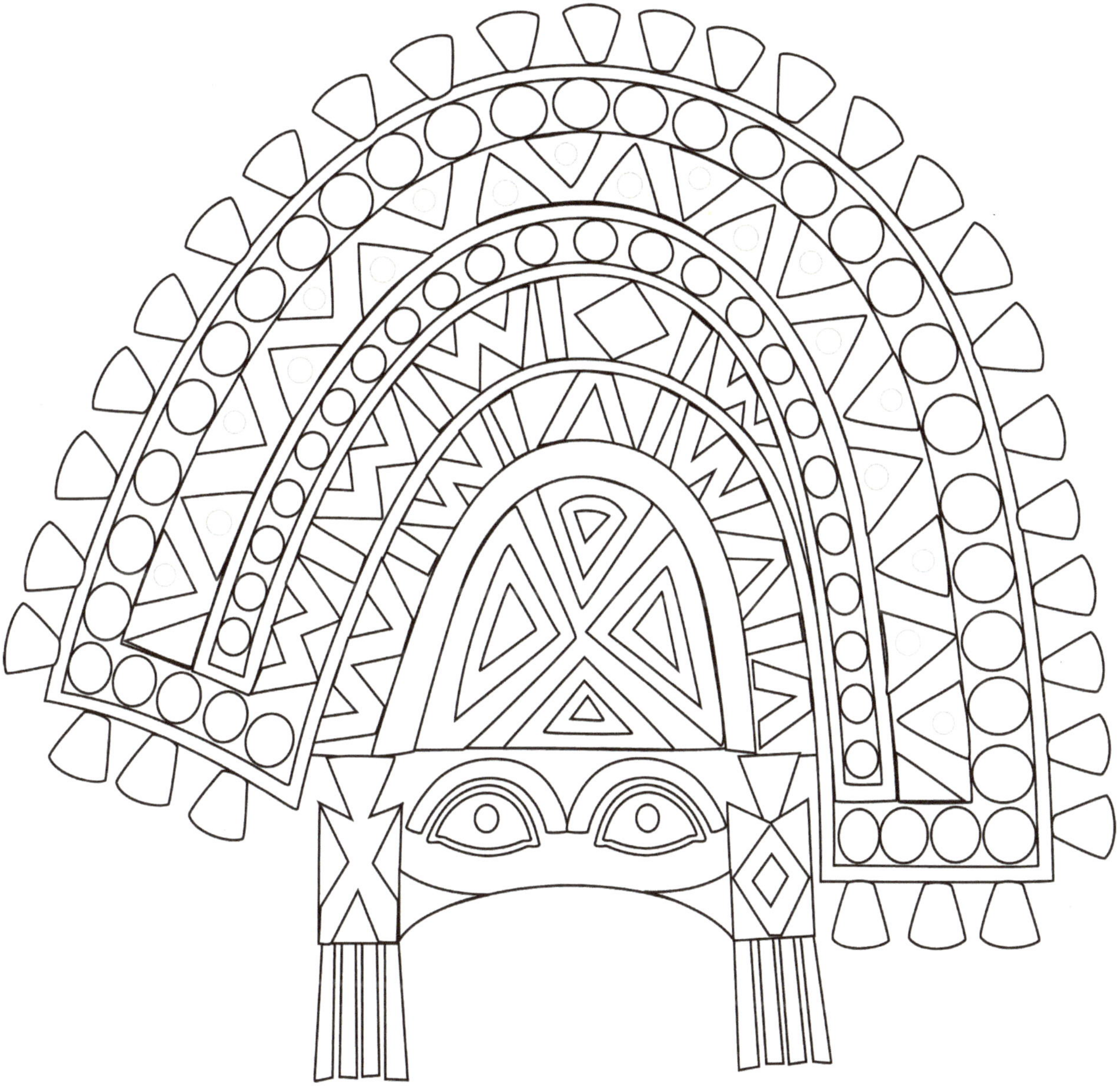

Color the drawing above using your preferred choice of colors.

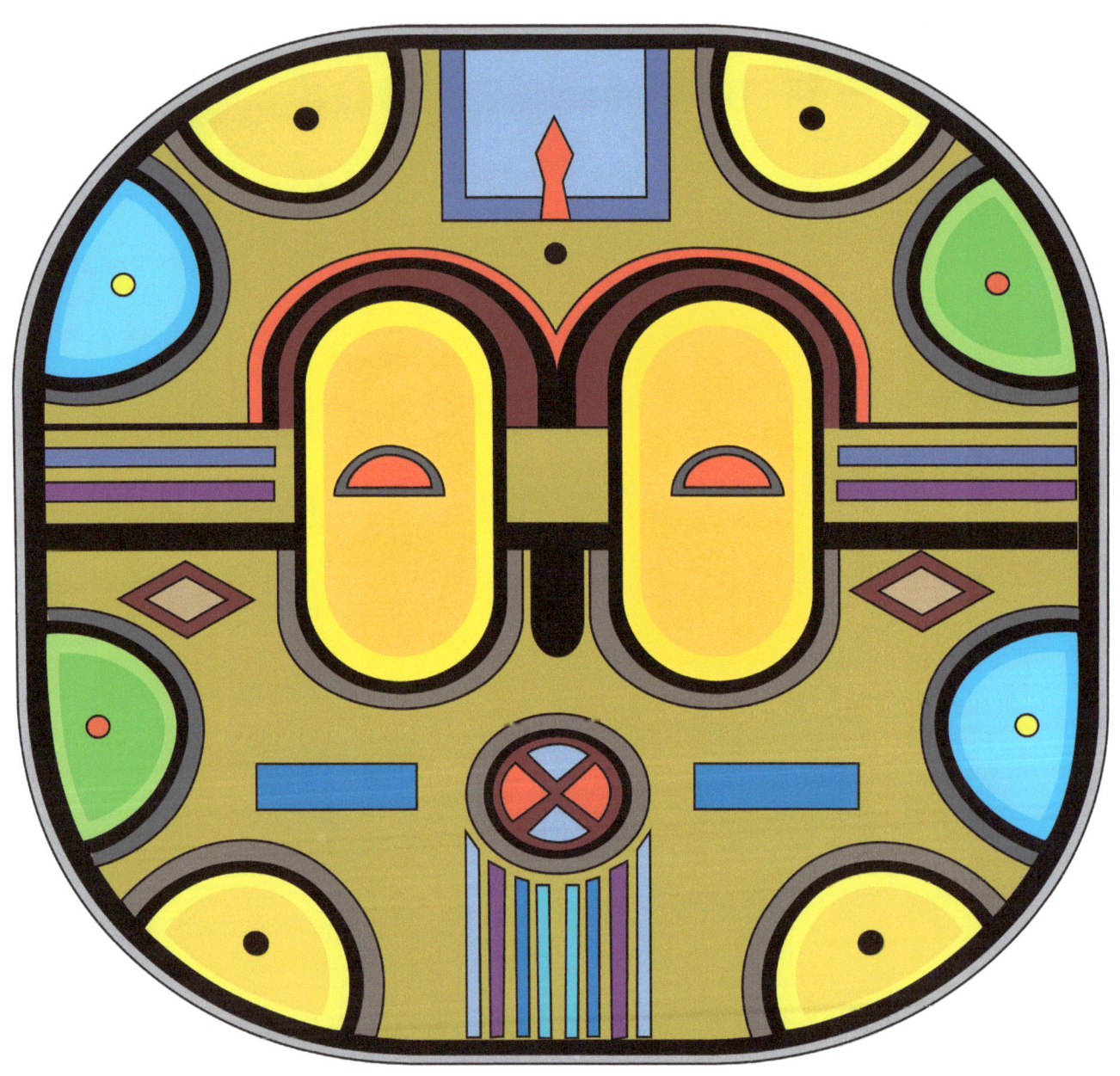

Teke Mask, from the Teke tribe of Congo. Hand carved on wood.
An abstraction of the human face. The nose and ear are prominent.

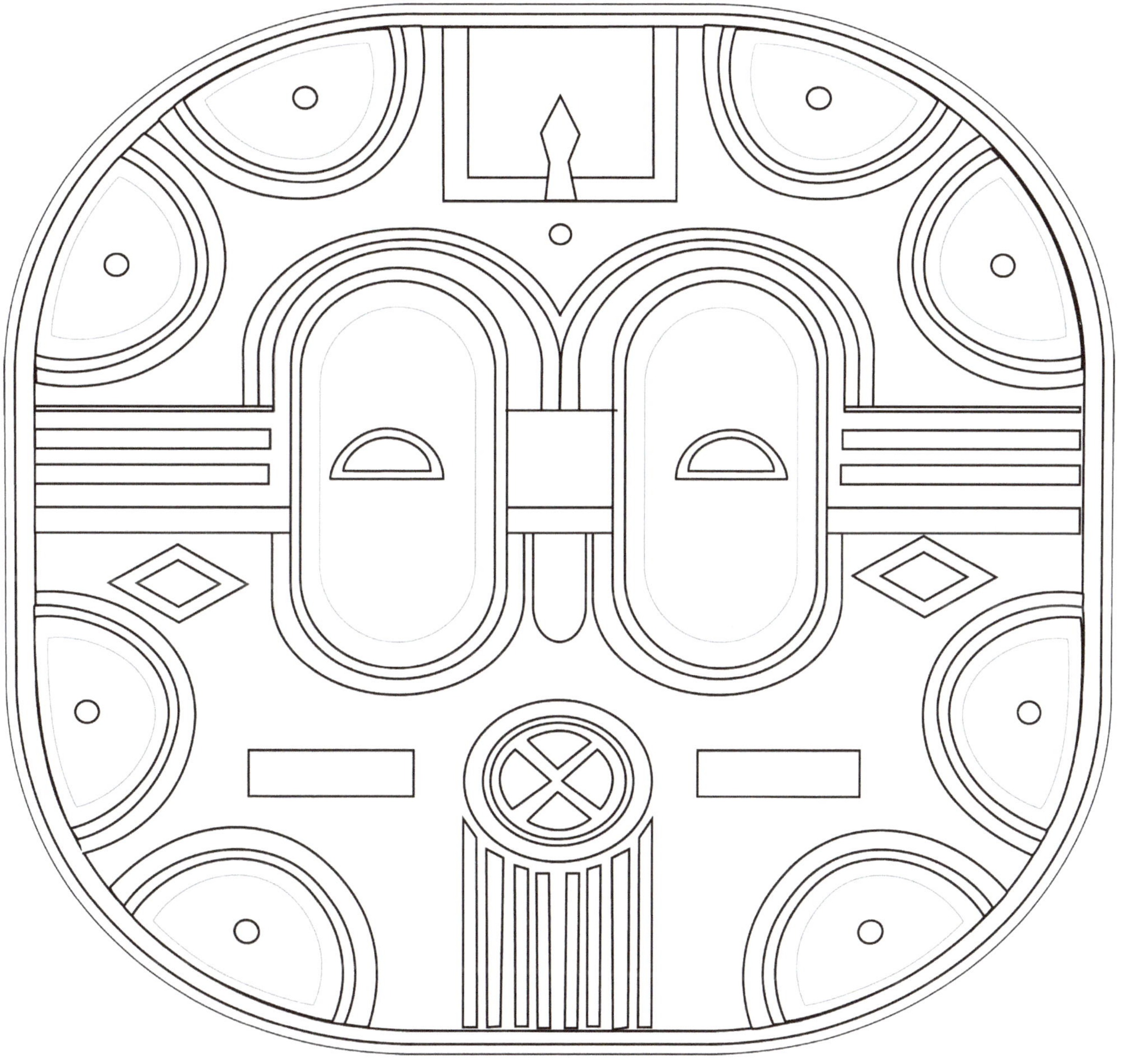

Color the drawing above using your preferred choice of colors.

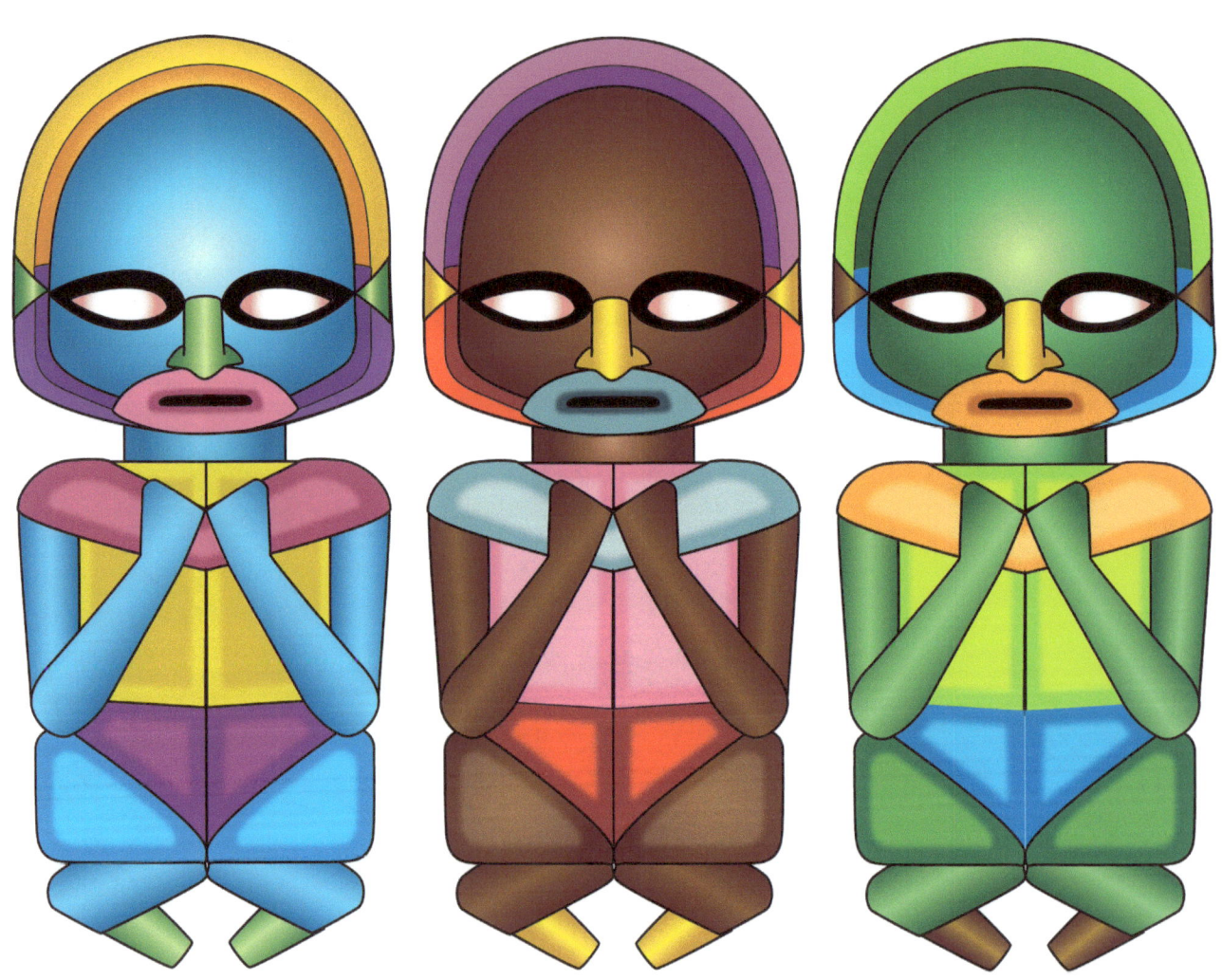

Initiation amulets. Woodwork. Bahungana, Congo.

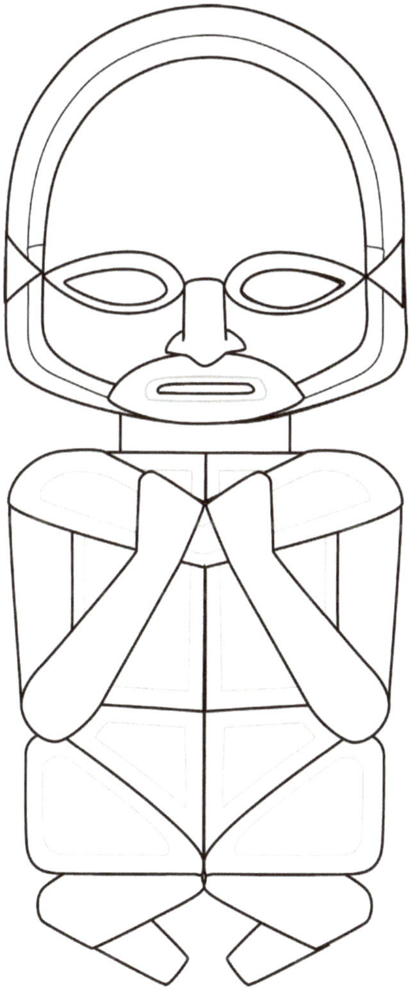

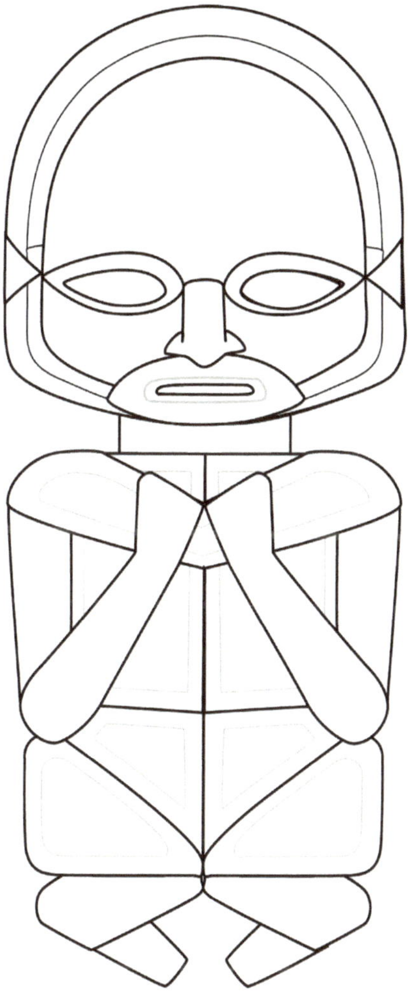

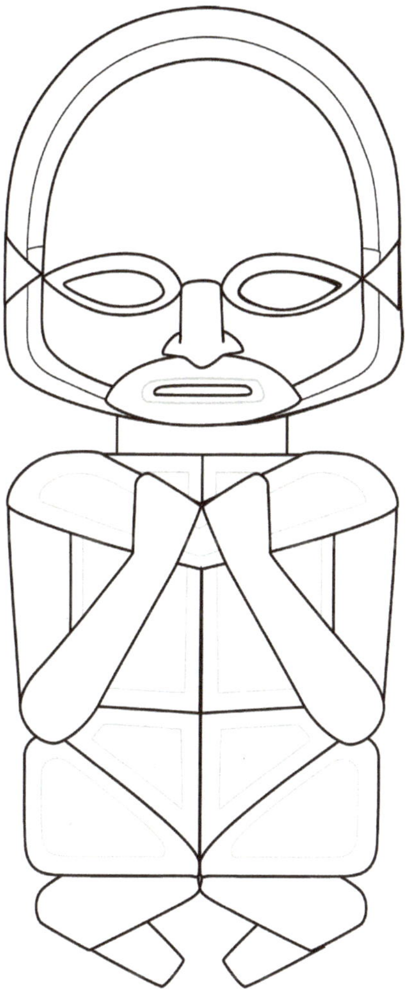

Color the drawings above using your preferred choice of colors.

25

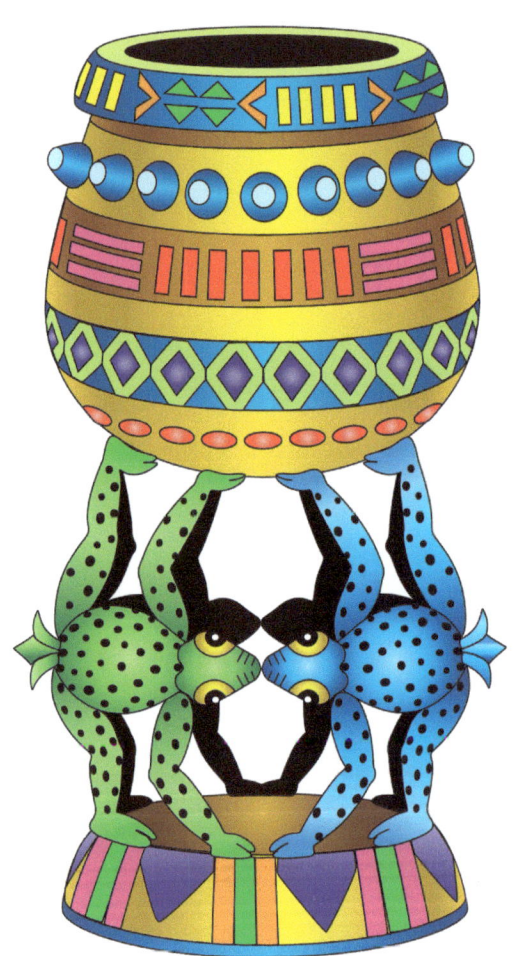

Oracle Bowl

Used to perform rituals, and to worship ancestors by Societies of Yoruba, Nigeria, and Mali.

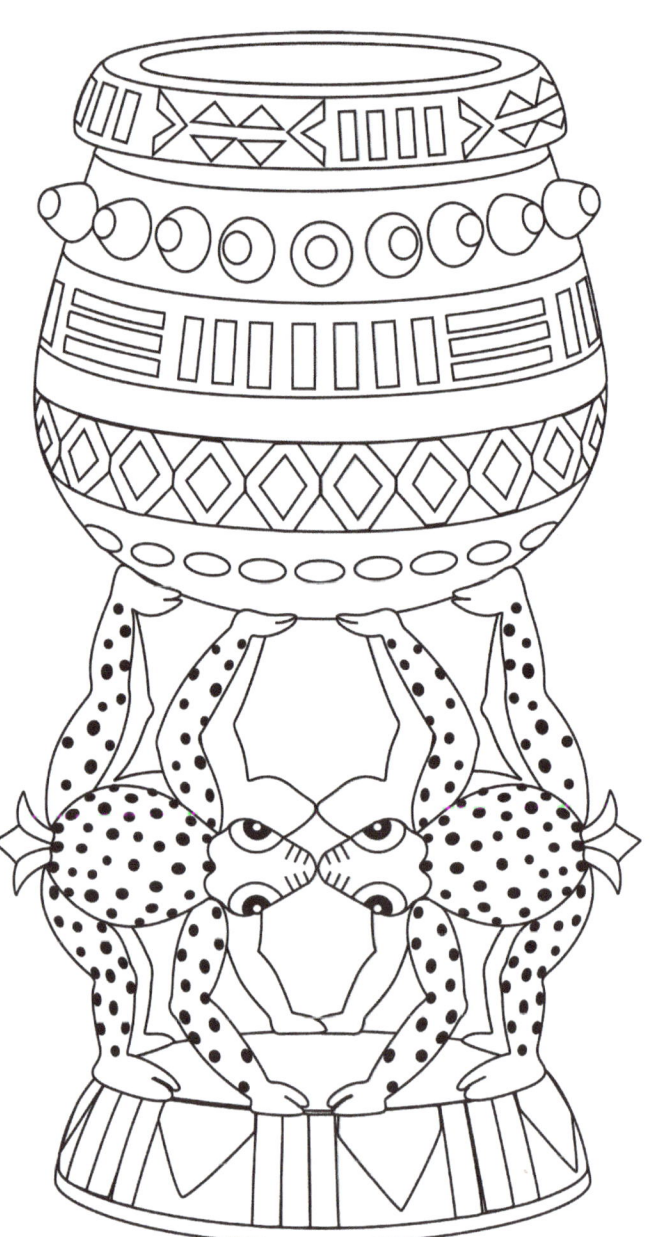

African Art

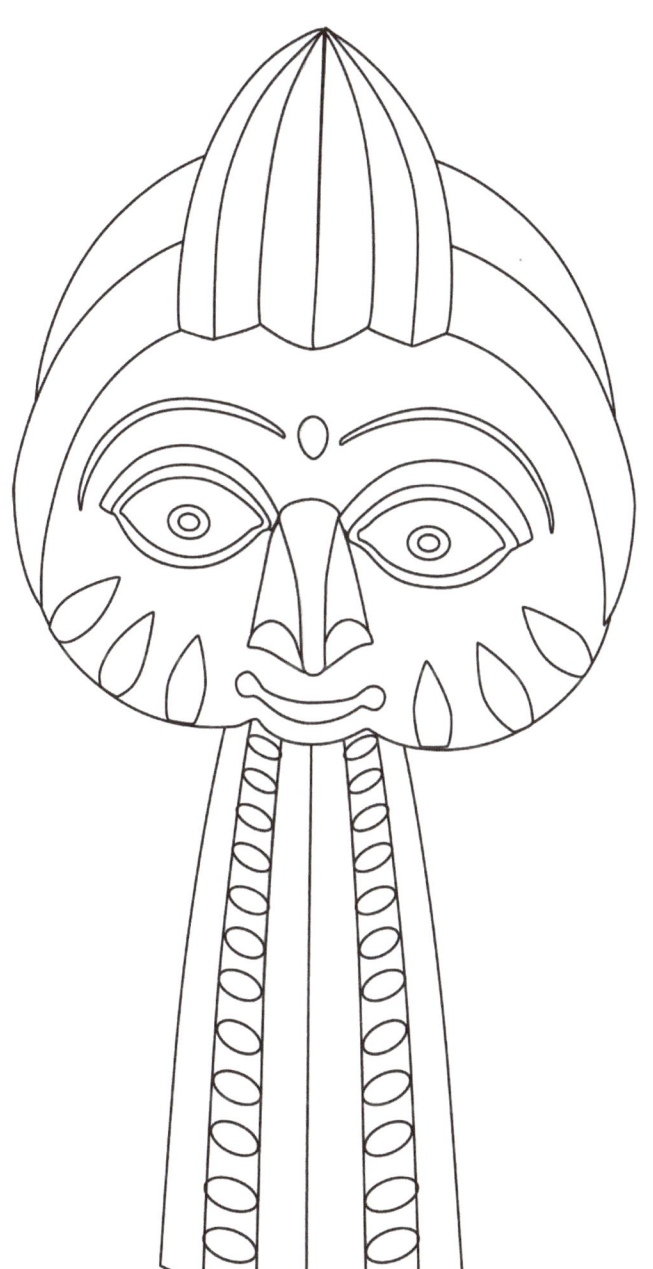

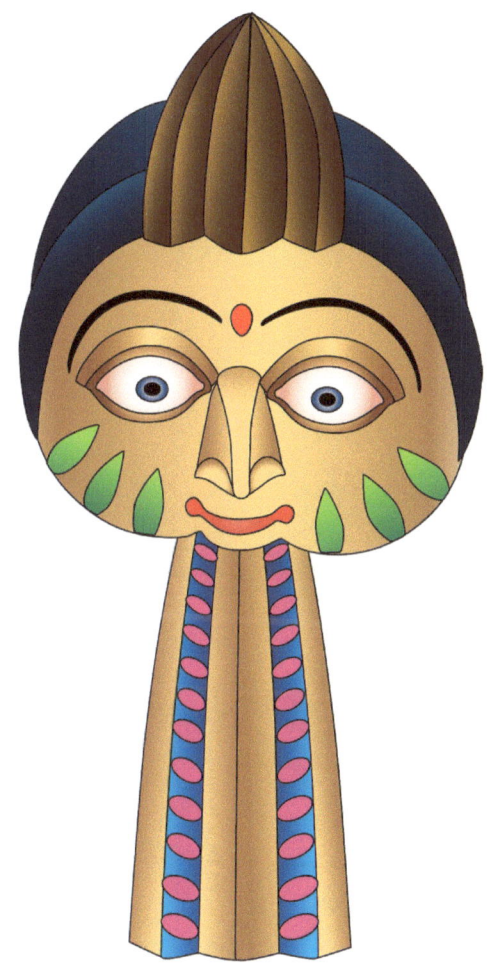

Yoruba Mask

The ritual takes place at the beginning of the agricultural season. The purpose is to pay tribute to the special power of women.

Color the drawings above using your preferred choice of colors.

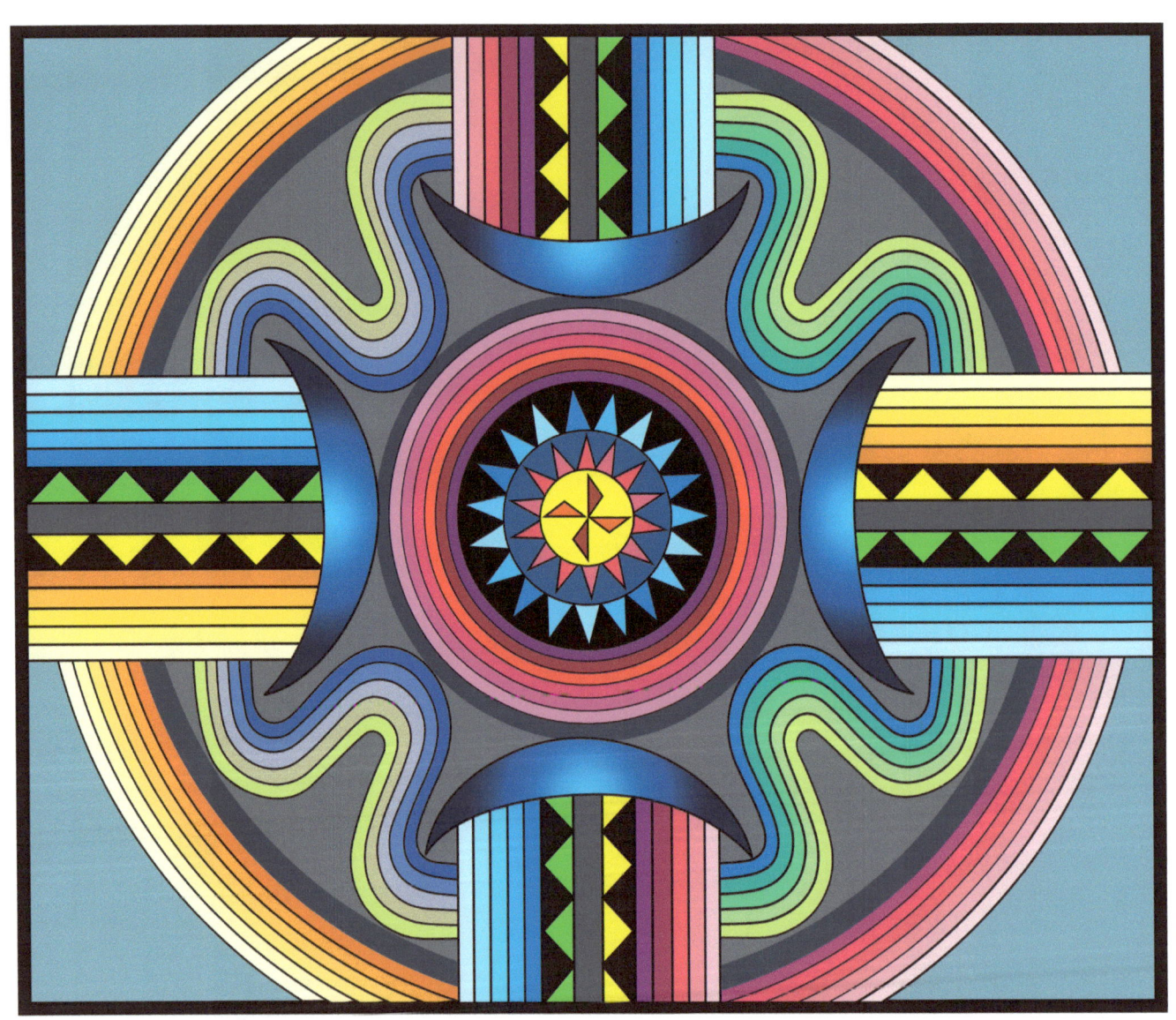

Designs and patterns are woven in silk Kente Cloth. Ashunti, Ghana.

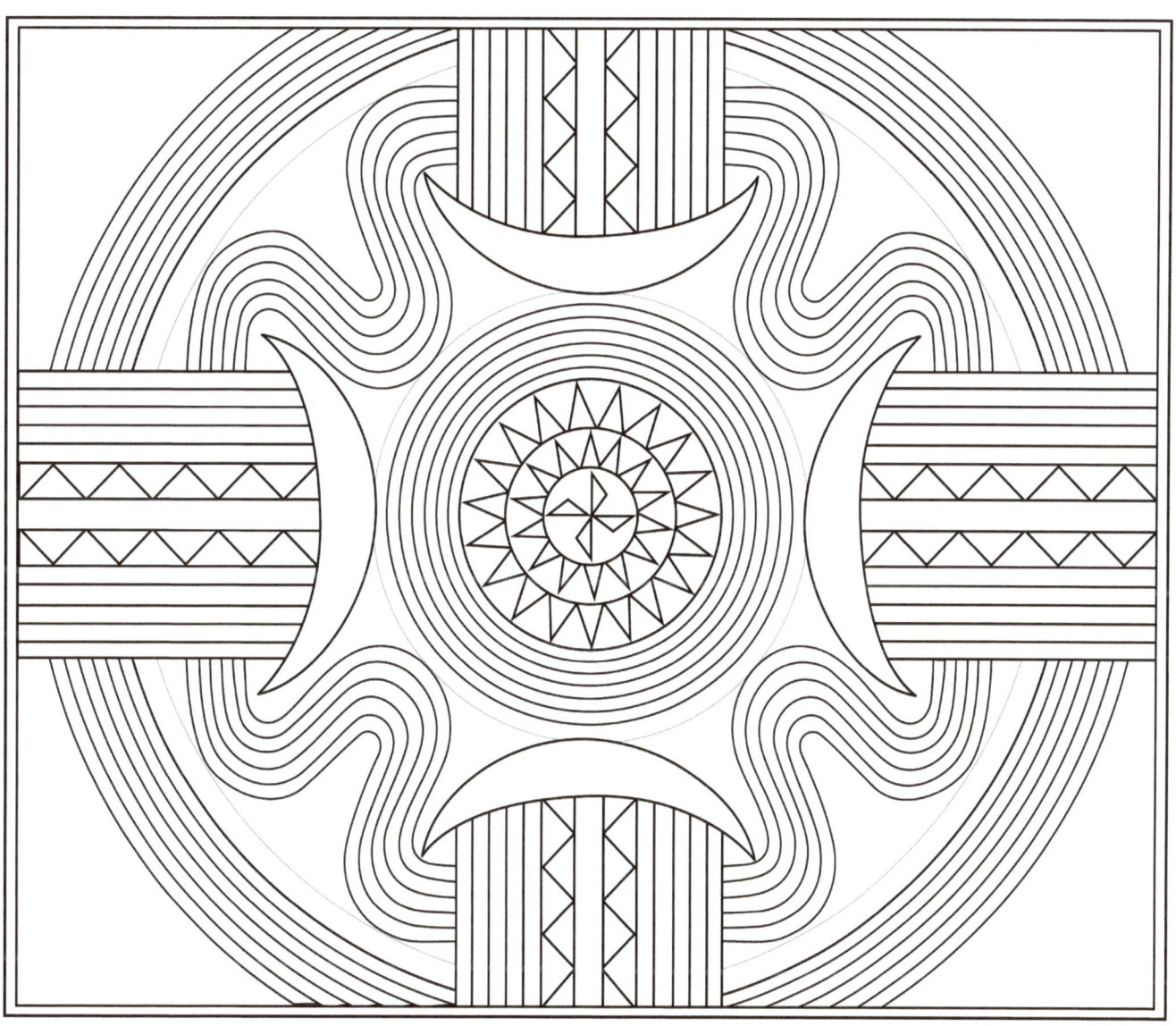

Color the drawing above using your preferred choice of colors.

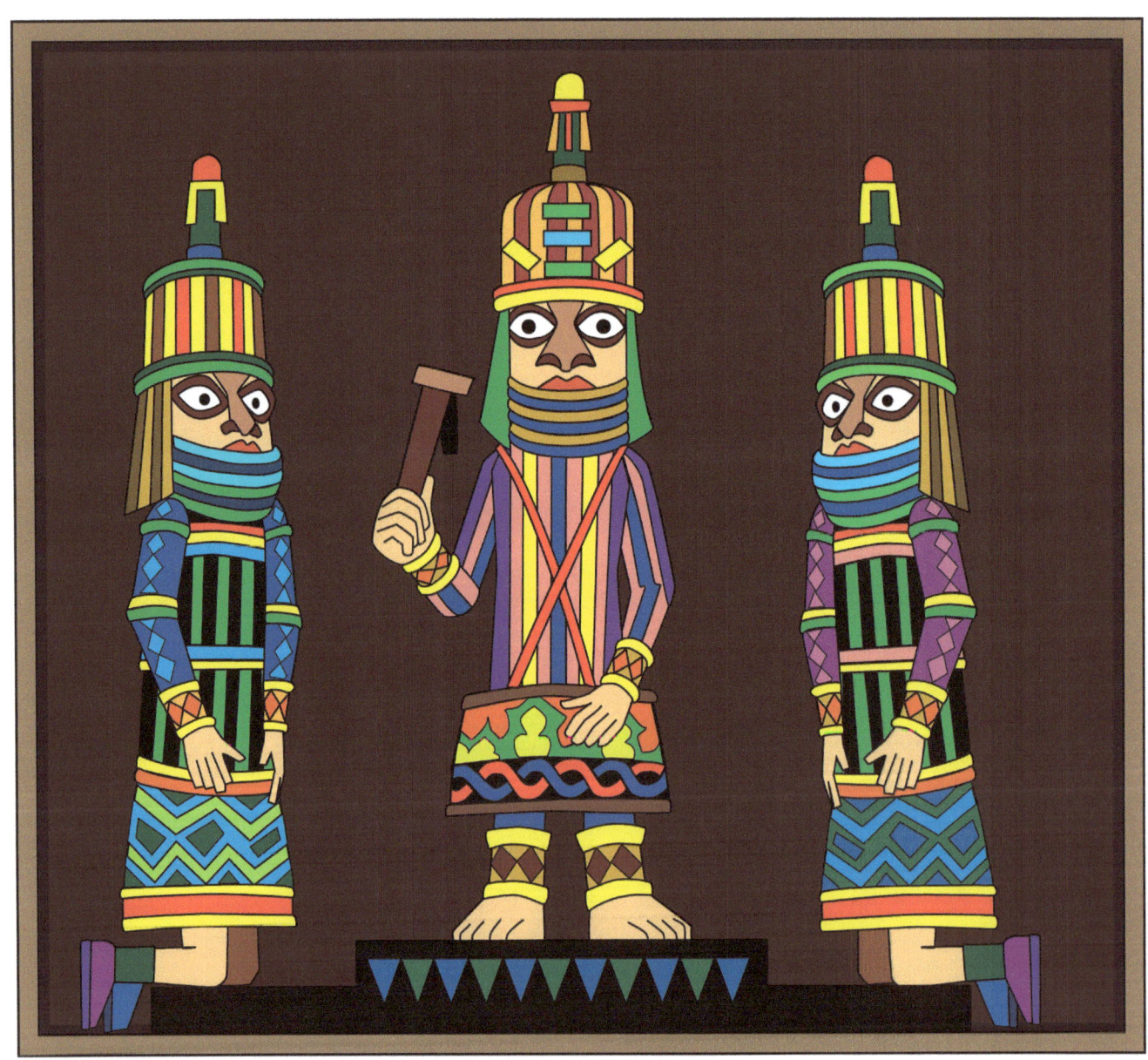

Bronze plaque, Benin, Nigeria. Made by Oba's special craftsmen to set forth his glory and power. 17th Century C.E.

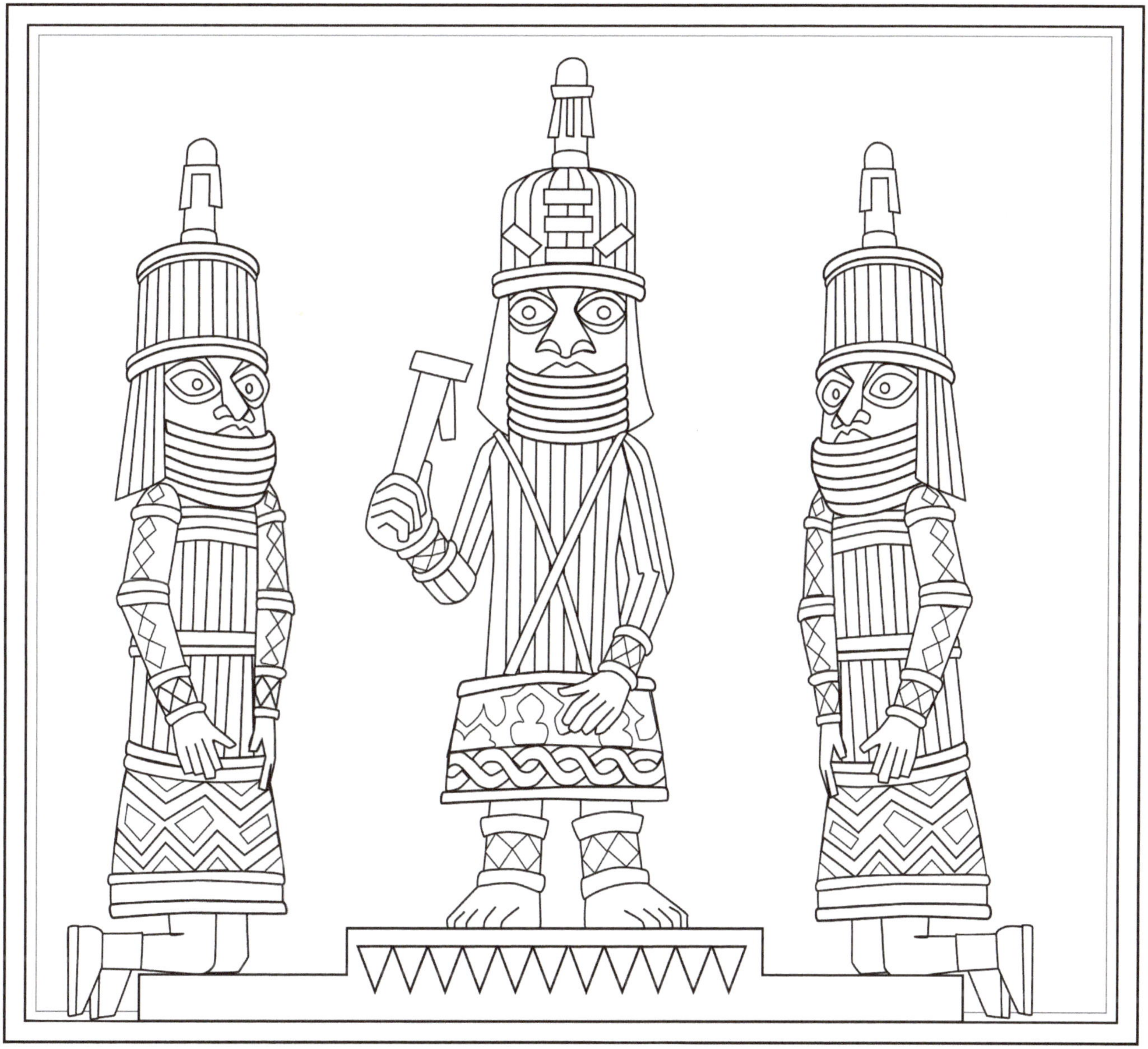

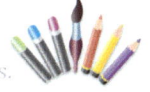

Color the drawing above using your preferred choice of colors.

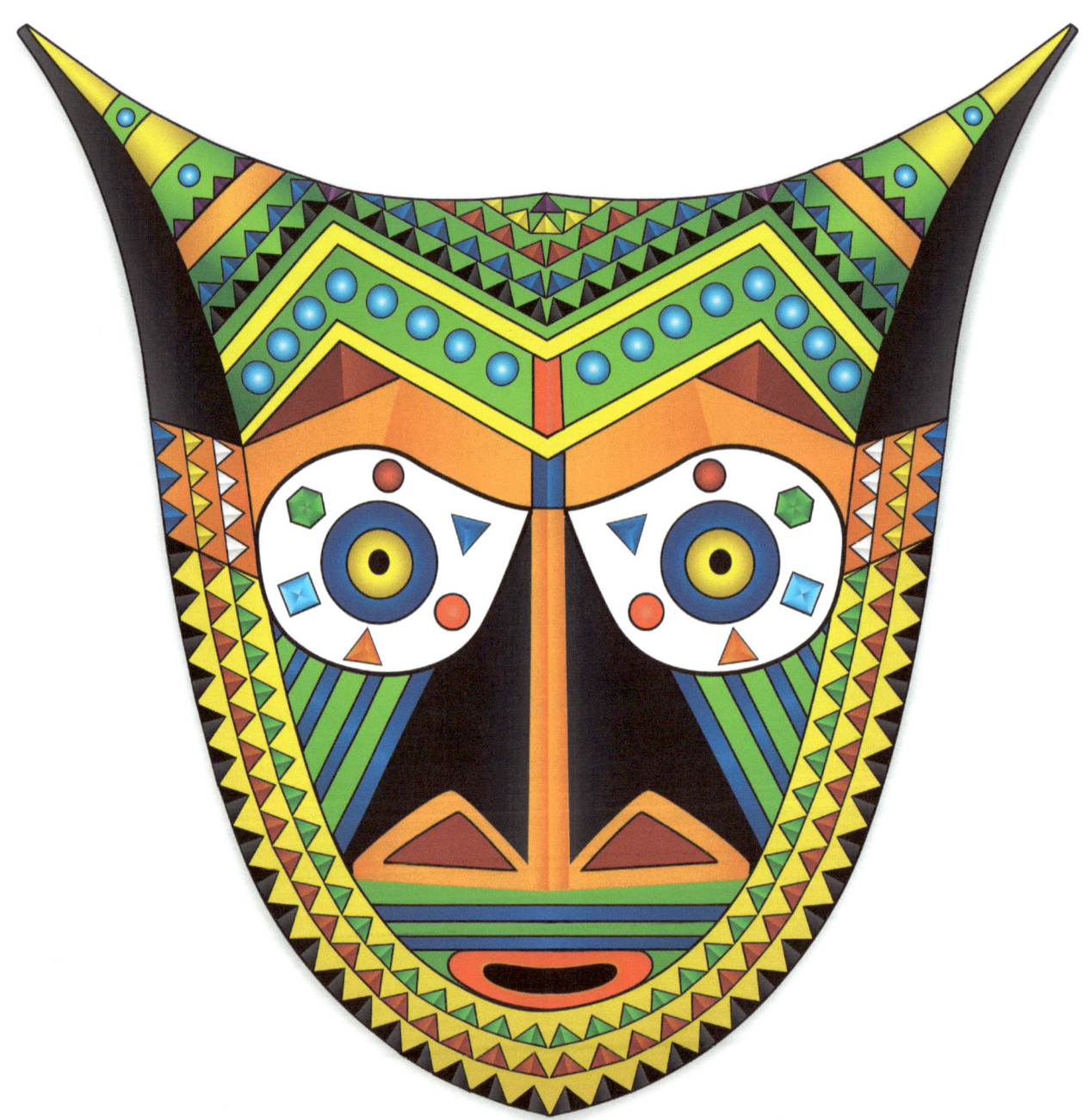

Dance mask, woodwork. Bakuba, Democratic Republic of the Congo.

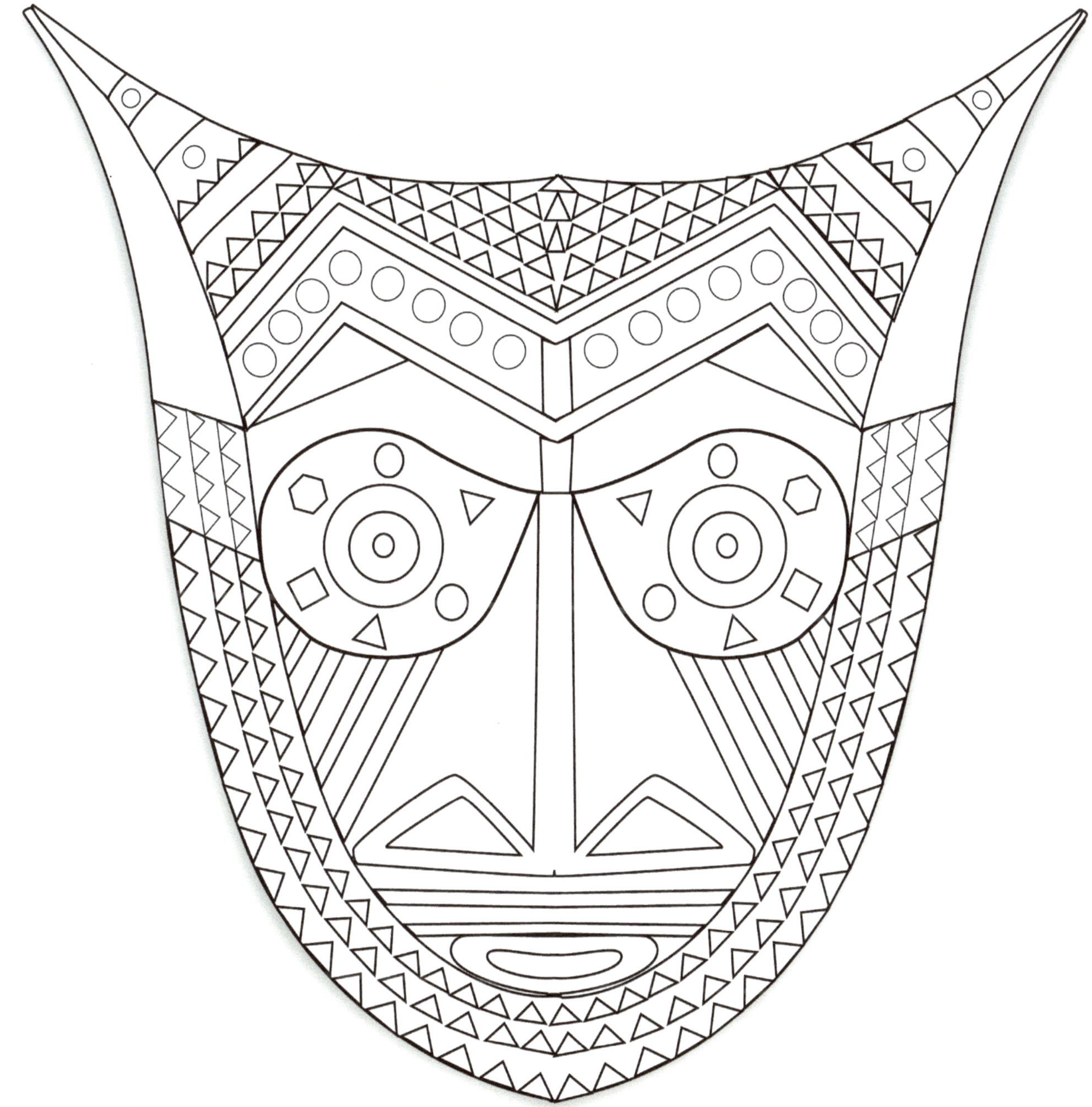

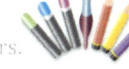

Color the drawing above using your preferred choice of colors.

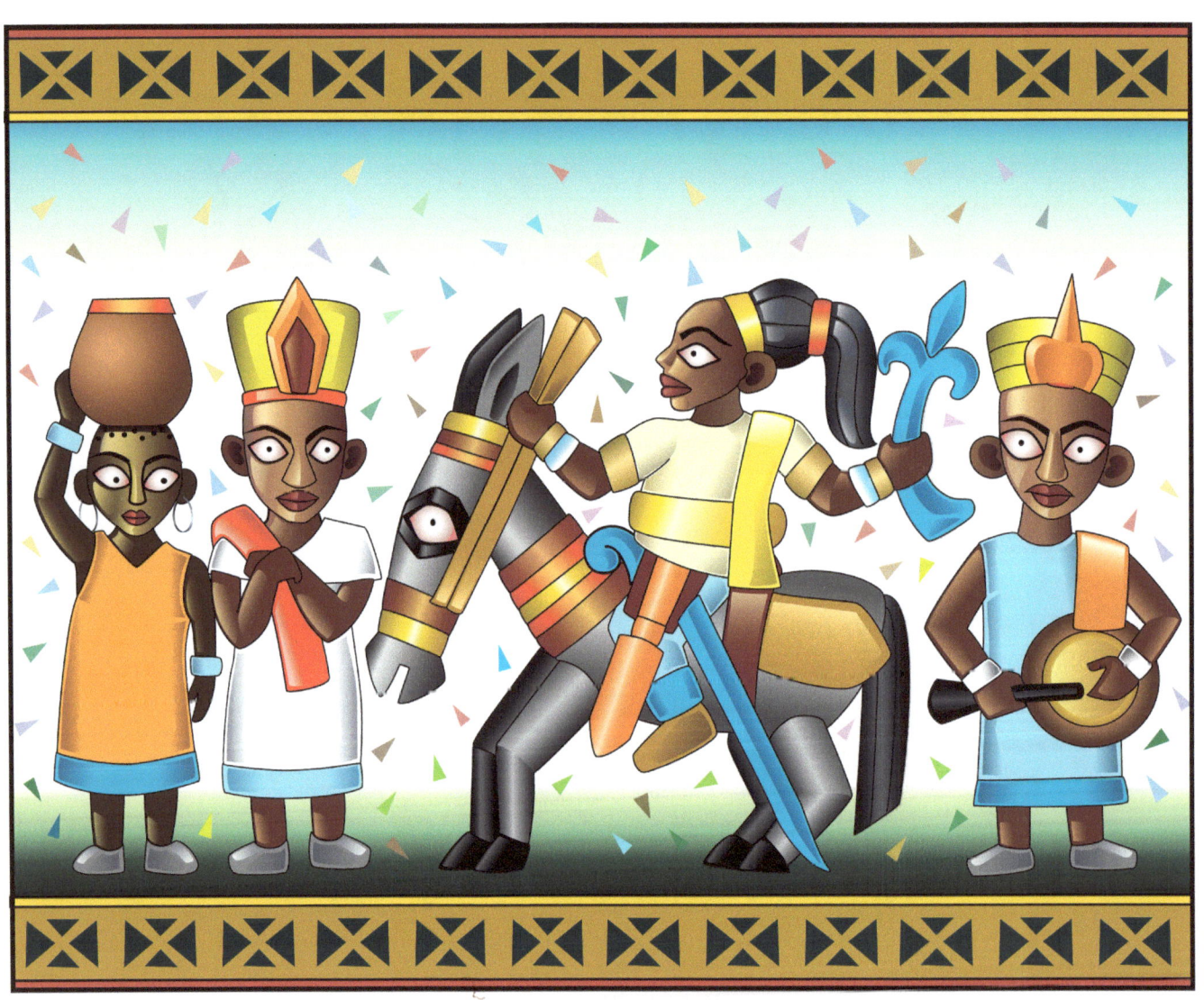

Part of Royal Procession from the frieze in the palace door in Yoruba, Nigeria.

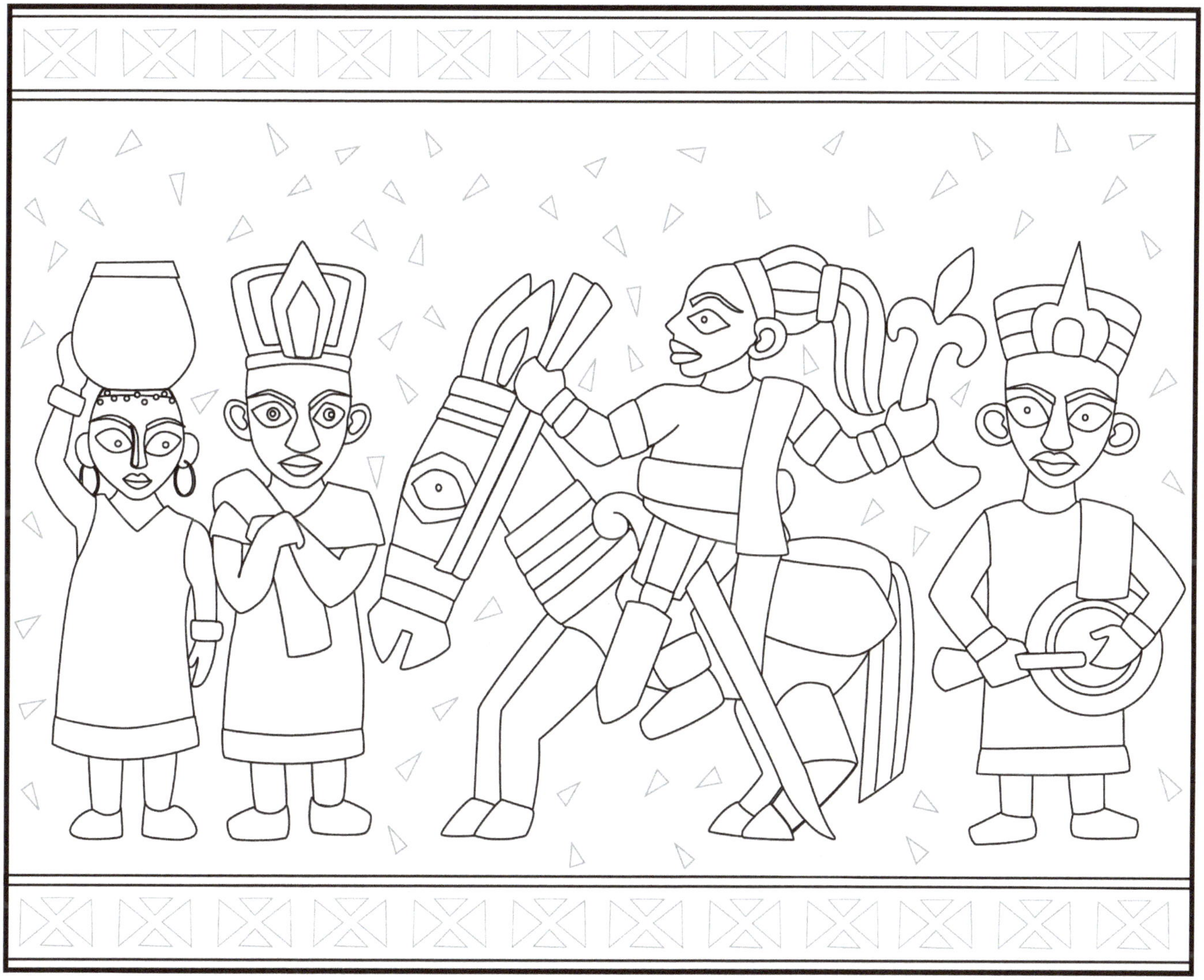

Color the drawing above using your preferred choice of colors.

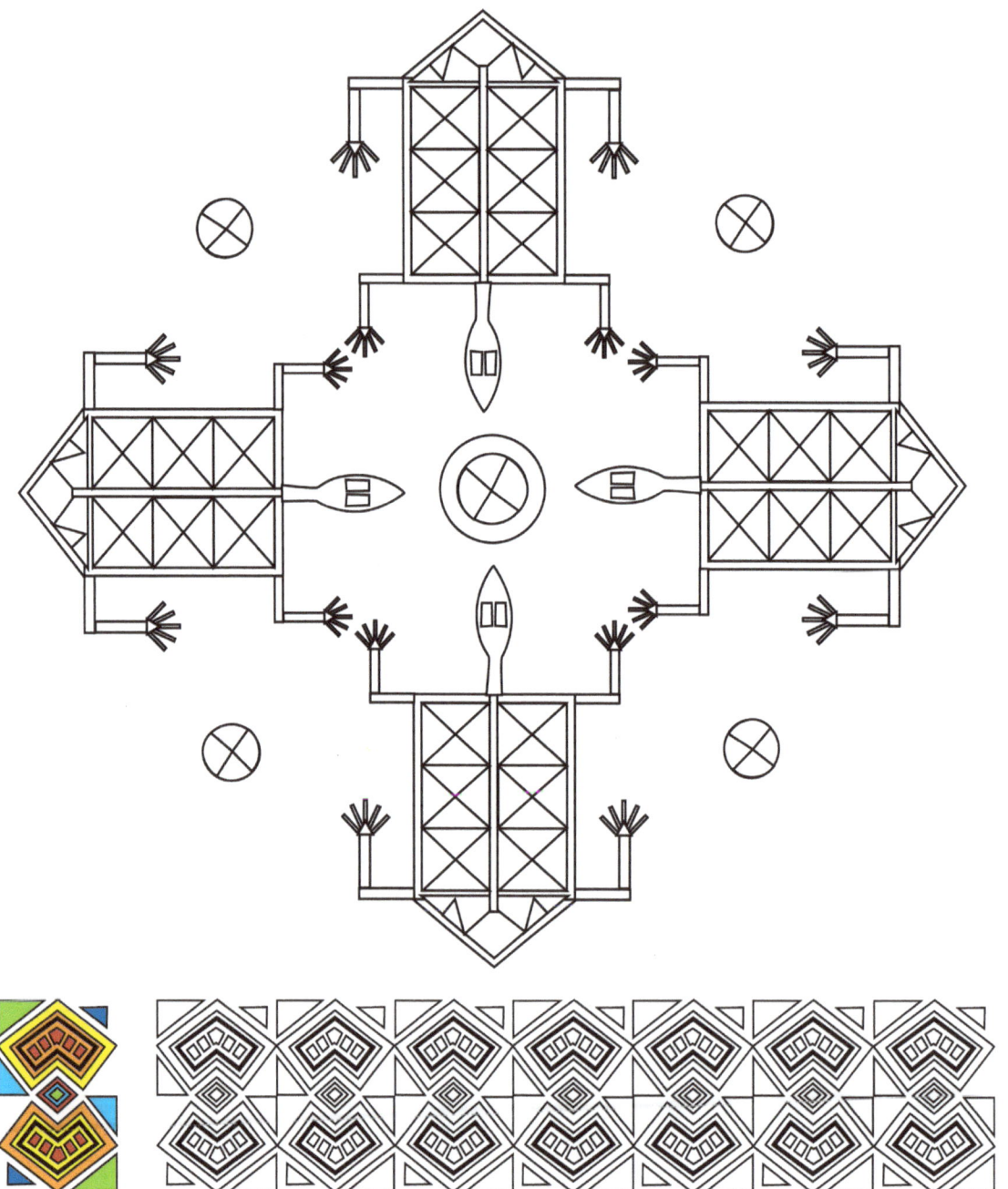

Using these images as examples, create your own piece using the elements found in African Art.

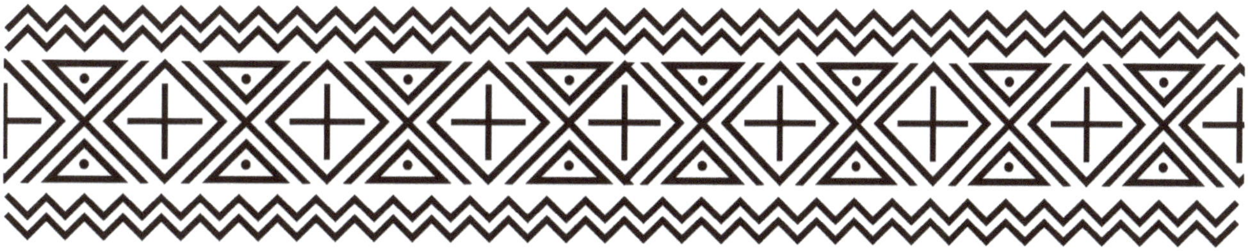

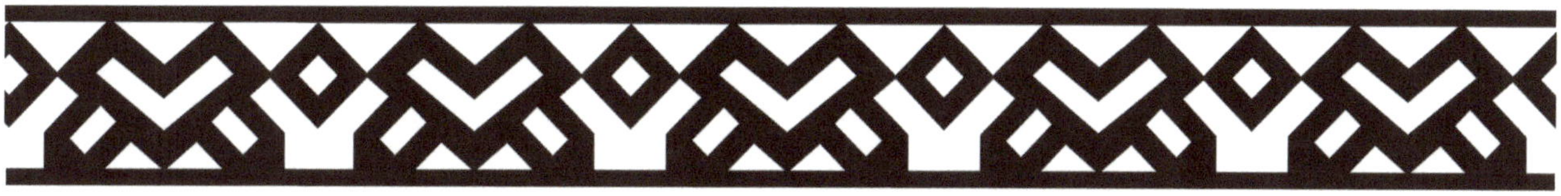

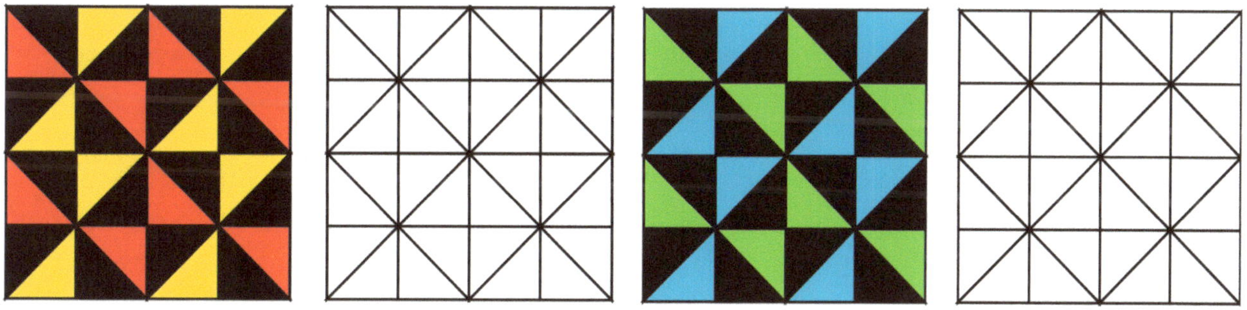

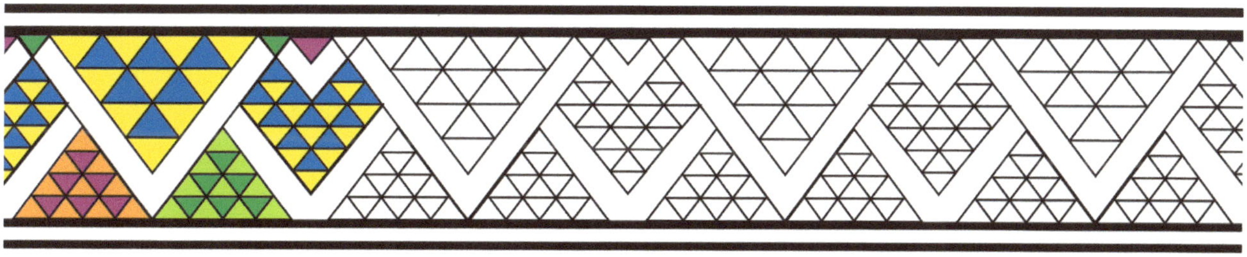

Color the drawings above using your preferred choice of colors.

= a synopsis of =
AFRICAN ART

The continent of Africa is filled with vibrant artistic cultures as well as incredible natural beauty. The term African art is typically used for the art of Sub-Saharan Africa. But recently, scholars and art historians have also included the arts of the African Diaspora found in Brazil, the Caribbean, and even in the United States. African Art in its entirety seemingly holds a unifying theme regardless of the diverse cultural differences found within the continent.

Countless of artists and connoisseurs are in awe with admiration of the sculptural qualities African Art possesses. Sculptures have been fashioned using various types of materials found in their local regions. The majority of the sculptures found were created with wood and from blocks of granite. Softer stones were used for carvings in Sierra Leone, Liberia, Yoruba Land, and in Lower Congo regions. Either mud or clay was used for the sculptures that were found on the solid walls.

Craftsmen carved logs into milk pots and other vessels, as well as into stools and headdresses. They even hollowed out tree trunks into canoes and made doors for their huts and granaries out of the thick planks. The art creators carved figurines and masks for religious and social ceremonies. Various forms of African art were made from different materials such as; haematite, sisal, coconut shells, beads, ebony wood, and so forth.

Pottery was customarily a woman's craft in Africa. Water pots and cooking vessels were coiled first and then roughly fired to maintain their shape. The life-size terracotta figures were made by men in northern Nigeria over two thousand years ago.

Tribal masks played an important role in the African indigenous community since the cultures are imbued with spirituality. Masks were worn in a variety of ways for festivals, initiation ceremonies, and secret societies. They were believed to represent a spirit who possessed the wearer.

OTHER TITLES IN THIS SERIES

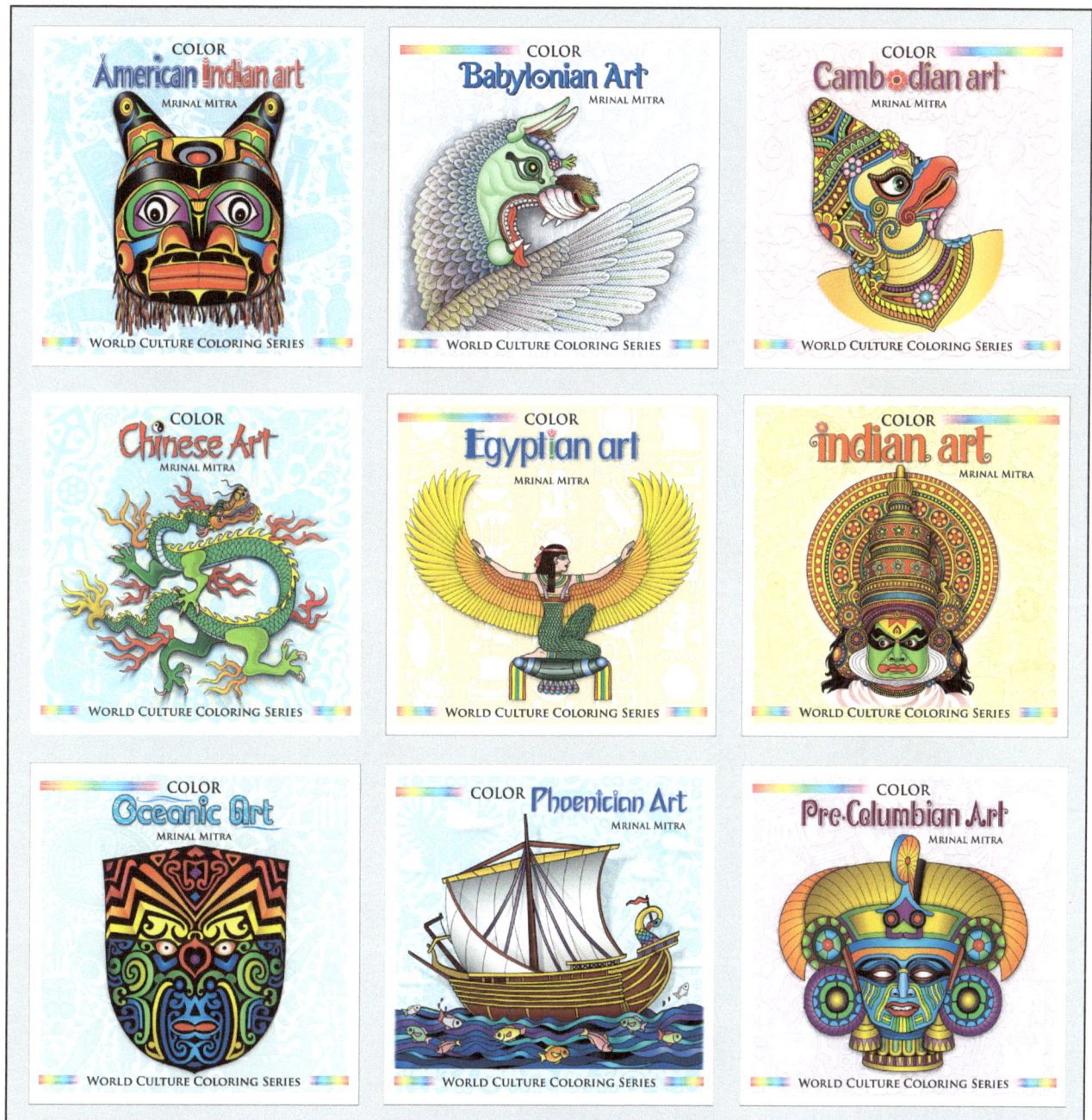

COLOR
American Indian Art
MRINAL MITRA
WORLD CULTURE COLORING SERIES

COLOR
Babylonian Art
MRINAL MITRA
WORLD CULTURE COLORING SERIES

COLOR
Cambodian Art
MRINAL MITRA
WORLD CULTURE COLORING SERIES

COLOR
Chinese Art
MRINAL MITRA
WORLD CULTURE COLORING SERIES

COLOR
Egyptian Art
MRINAL MITRA
WORLD CULTURE COLORING SERIES

COLOR
Indian Art
MRINAL MITRA
WORLD CULTURE COLORING SERIES

COLOR
Oceanic Art
MRINAL MITRA
WORLD CULTURE COLORING SERIES

COLOR
Phoenician Art
MRINAL MITRA
WORLD CULTURE COLORING SERIES

COLOR
Pre-Columbian Art
MRINAL MITRA
WORLD CULTURE COLORING SERIES

AVAILABLE FROM AMAZON.COM, CREATESPACE.COM, AND OTHER RETAIL OUTLETS

Acknowledgement

First and foremost, this series would not be possible without the number of great historical art found within the different cultural regions around the world.

In addition, we would like to acknowledge the variety of publishing's from all over the world for allowing us to learn about their fascinating ancestral art and culture. With this provided knowledge, we have hoped to have represented the art as splendidly as you have supplied it.

About the Author

Mrinal Mitra has earned a number of prestigious awards, both Indian and International, and received honors for his outstanding illustrations. Some of his recognitions include; The Noma Concours Award, Japan (twice), Illustrators Award, and Children's Choice Award, India, and honors from German Television "Transtel", BRNO- CSSR, TIBI- Iran, and UNICEF, New York.

Many of his talented artworks have been exhibited in several different countries such as; India, Japan, Italy, Czech Republic, Iran, and New Zealand. Mitra has authored, designed and illustrated trade and educational children's books for many Indian as well as Multinational Book Publishers around the globe.

Copyright: Mrinal Mitra, 2014

www.ingramcontent.com/pod-product-compliance
Lightning Source LLC
Chambersburg PA
CBHW050839180526
45159CB00004B/1966